DEAN KOONTZ

Recent Titles in
Critical Companions to Popular Contemporary Writers
Kathleen Gregory Klein, Series Editor

DEAN KOONTZ

A Critical Companion

Joan G. Kotker

CRITICAL COMPANIONS TO POPULAR CONTEMPORARY WRITERS
Kathleen Gregory Klein, Series Editor

Greenwood Press
Westport, Connecticut • London

Library of Congress Cataloging-in-Publication Data

Kotker, Joan G.
    Dean Koontz : a critical companion / Joan G. Kotker.
      p. cm.—(Critical companions to popular contemporary
writers, ISSN 1082–4979)
    Includes bibliographical references (p.   ) and index.
    ISBN 0–313–29528–X (alk. paper)
    1. Koontz, Dean R. (Dean Ray), 1945– —Criticism and
interpretation. 2. Horror tales, American—History and criticism.
I. Title. II. Series.
PS3561.055Z74 1996
813'.54—dc20   96–2547

British Library Cataloguing in Publication Data is available.

Library of Congress Catalog Card Number: 96–2547
ISBN: 0–313–29528–X
ISSN: 1082–4979

First published in 1996

Greenwood Press, 88 Post Road West, Westport, CT 06881
An imprint of Greenwood Publishing Group, Inc.

Printed in the United States of America

The paper used in this book complies with the
Permanent Paper Standard issued by the National
Information Standards Organization (Z39.48–1984).

10 9 8 7 6 5 4 3 2 1

Contents

Series Foreword

The authors who appear in the series Critical Companions to Popular Contemporary Writers are all best-selling writers. They do not have only one successful novel, but a string of them. Fans, critics, and specialist readers eagerly anticipate their next book. For some, high cash advances and breakthrough sales figures are automatic; movie deals often follow. Some writers become household names, recognized by almost everyone.

But novels are read one by one. Each reader chooses to start and, more importantly, to finish a book because of what she or he finds there. The real test of a novel is in the satisfaction its readers experience. This series acknowledges the extraordinary involvement of readers and writers in creating a best-seller.

The authors included in this series were chosen by an Advisory Board composed of high school English teachers and high school and public librarians. They ranked a list of best-selling writers according to their popularity among different groups of readers. Writers in the top-ranked group who had not received book-length, academic literary analysis (or none in at least the past ten years) were chosen for the series. Because of this selection method, Critical Companions to Popular Contemporary Writers meets a need that is not addressed elsewhere.

The volumes in the series are written by scholars with particular expertise in analyzing popular fiction. These specialists add an academic focus to the popular success that the best-selling writers already enjoy.

The series is designed to appeal to a wide range of readers. The general reading public will find explanations for the appeal of these well-known writers. Fans will find biographical and fictional questions answered. Students will find literary analysis, discussions of fictional genres, carefully organized introductions to new ways of reading the novels, and bibliographies for additional research. Students will also be able to apply what they have learned from this book to their readings of future novels by these best-selling writers.

Each volume begins with a biographical chapter drawing on published information, autobiographies or memoirs, prior interviews, and, in some cases, interviews given especially for this series. A chapter on literary history and genres describes how the author's work fits into a larger literary context. The following chapters analyze the writer's most important, most popular, and most recent novels in detail. Each chapter focuses on a single novel. This approach, suggested by the Advisory Board as the most useful to student research, allows for an in-depth analysis of the writer's fiction. Close and careful readings with numerous examples show readers exactly how the novels work. These chapters are organized around three central elements: plot development (how the story line moves forward), character development (what the reader knows about the important figures), and theme (the significant ideas of the novel). Chapters may also include sections on generic conventions (how the novel is similar to or different from others in its same category of science fiction, fantasy, thriller, etc.), narrative point of view (who tells the story and how), symbols and literary language, and historical or social context. Each chapter ends with an "alternative reading" of the novel. The volume concludes with a primary and secondary bibliography, including reviews.

The Alternative Readings are a unique feature of this series. By demonstrating a particular way of reading each novel, they provide a clear example of how a specific perspective can reveal important aspects of the book. In each alternative reading section, one contemporary literary theory—such as feminist criticism, Marxism, new historicism, deconstruction, or Jungian psychological critique—is defined in brief, easily comprehensible language. That definition is then applied to the novel to highlight specific features that might go unnoticed or be understood differently in a more general reading of the novel. Each volume defines two or three specific theories, making them part of the reader's understanding of how diverse meanings may be constructed from a single novel.

Taken collectively, the volumes in the Critical Companions to Popular Contemporary Writers series provide a wide-ranging investigation of the complexities of current best-selling fiction. By treating these novels seriously as both literary works and publishing successes, the series demonstrates the potential of popular literature in contemporary culture.

Kathleen Gregory Klein
Southern Connecticut State University

1

The Life of Dean Koontz

FAMILY BACKGROUND AND EDUCATION

Dean Ray Koontz was born in Everett, Pennsylvania, on July 9, 1945, the only child of Ray and Florence Koontz. He grew up in Bedford, Pennsylvania, a town of 4,000 in the central, rural hill country of the state. He was educated at Shippensburg State College in Pennsylvania, where he majored in English and minored in communications, and he worked as a teacher-counsellor in the Appalachian Poverty Program and as a high school English teacher before becoming the full-time writer that he is today. His first novel, *Star Quest*, was published in 1968 and since then he has published a total of sixty novels, using both his own name and ten pseudonyms. In 1966 Koontz was awarded the *Atlantic Monthly* Creative Writing Award for his short story "Kittens," and in 1971 his novella, *Beastchild*, received a Hugo Award nomination. He is a member of Mystery Writers of America and Horror Writers of America, and is married to the former Gerda Ann Cerra. He lives in the Newport-Laguna area of California.

Dean Koontz's childhood was one that no child should be forced to endure. The family was very poor, and this was primarily because of the character of Koontz's father, Ray, an alcoholic who was violent when he was drunk and who, not surprisingly, lost one job after another because of his drinking. Although the father was relatively short—5'6"—he must have seemed huge to a small child, and it is likely that his drunken rages have contributed a great deal to such terrifying sociopathic characters as Bruno Frye in *Whispers* (see Chapter 8), The Outsider in *Watchers* (see Chapter 5), and Alfie in *Mr. Murder* (see Chapter 9). All three are characters consumed by a need for violence. Another contributing factor to the poverty of Koontz's childhood was the fact that his father was a compulsive gambler, so that even when Ray Koontz was employed (he was a salesman, and Koontz says that he was a good one), there was no guarantee that his family would benefit. In later life, Ray Koontz was diagnosed as borderline schizophrenic with tendencies to violence complicated by alcoholism, and throughout his son's life, he continued to be a real danger to him, attacking the adult Dean twice with a knife in an attempt to kill him.

People magazine, in a 1994 interview with Koontz, ran a picture of the house he grew up in, a graphic representation of the deprivation of his childhood. A four-room house built (poorly, Koontz says) by his grandfather, it is a classic portrait of rural poverty. In fact, it was not until the writer was about ten years old that the house had indoor plumbing, and this would have been in about 1955, when most middle-class American homes were anticipating their first television sets rather than their first indoor toilets. Koontz says of this time, "We were always on the edge of destitution and my father was a violent drunk. . . . You have nowhere to go when you grow up in a household like that" (Feeney and Gleick 1994, 142). Somehow, though, Dean Koontz found a place to go—in his writing.

If Dean Koontz was cursed in terms of the father fate gave him, he was blessed in his mother. She was a very pretty woman, small and delicate; in her picture in *People*, she looks like the actress Wynona Ryder. Koontz has described her as a gentle, passive woman who was also very brave, and he credits her with shielding him from much of his father's rage. She is clearly the source of the many fine women characters Koontz uses in his works—women who are beaten down by circumstances and who yet find the strength to go on and create better lives for themselves and their children. One of the most vividly imagined of these women is Janet Marco of *Dragon Tears* (1993), a homeless woman who lives in a car with her five-year-old son Danny and scavenges in the affluent Laguna area of California, "seeking survival in the discards of others" (44).

Koontz shows, through the character of Janet, the tension and despair of living in poverty, of having no resources, nothing to fall back on if things should go wrong, if something out of the ordinary should occur.

He describes her terror of having something happen to her old car, a battered Dodge: "She lived in dread of a mechanical breakdown severe enough to be irreparable—or irreparable within their means, which was the same thing. But she was most afraid of theft, because with the car gone they would have no roof over their heads, no safe place to sleep" (45). The image of a car as a safe place to sleep—indeed, as safe place to live—shows vividly the vulnerability of Janet and Danny.

Janet is the child of sadistic alcoholics (as is Holly Thorne of 1991's *Cold Fire*—see Chapter 7—who is another strong female protagonist). In her effort to escape these parents, Janet married Vince Marco, a man who seemed strong and who turned out to be a wife-beater and control freak. His name is very similar to that of Vince Nasco, the psychopathic contract killer in *Watchers*, who seeks immortality; in some ways, Nasco has attained this, since characters like him appear over and over again in Koontz's work. It is as though Koontz has conferred a kind of fictional immortality on both his mother and father, showing his mother's goodness and courage through many of his female protagonists or heroes and his father's sadism and pathology through many of his male antagonists or villains.

Overall, in terms of Koontz's positive image of women, it is unusual to find female antagonists in Koontz's work, and when they do appear, they are partnered with a male antagonist who is the dominant figure, as in the parents of Janet. In *Dragon Tears*, Janet ends up killing Vince to protect Danny, who was at that time only four years old. She flees to California with the boy in the old Dodge, and there is a strong hint that Vince's body will never be discovered and she will never be charged with the crime. It is when she is in California that the reader is introduced to her in the novel. In her killing of Vince, Janet is the most extreme portrait of Koontz's passive female characters, who somehow find within themselves the strength to strike out against their fates. It is tempting to see in them the ultimate triumph of the young, pretty Florence Koontz, who found in herself the strength to protect her son.

BEGINNINGS AS A WRITER

When Dean Koontz looks back at his almost-textbook example of a dysfunctional family and considers what it was that enabled him to escape, he credits his mother and the world of his imagination. From an early age he loved books, movies, and cartoon figures, and these too appear with regularity in his work, enabling the characters in them to envision other worlds for themselves in the same way as they enabled the young Koontz to do so. He was especially fond of Donald Duck and Uncle Scrooge comics, and he has given this fondness to one of his most beloved characters, Einstein, the dog in *Watchers*. Other cartoon figures appear in such works as 1990's *The Bad Place* (see Chapter 8), and whenever they appear, they bring at least a moment of innocence and happiness to their surroundings. If Dean Koontz was a child who loved stories in any form, whether on film, in books, or in comics, he was also a child who loved to tell stories. From about the age of eight, he wrote his own books and sold them to relatives for five cents each. It would be a fortunate Dean Koontz relative who still had one of those early works.

Koontz left home after high school and went to Shippensburg State College, where he majored in English and minored in communications. While he was a student there, a story he wrote for a class won the coveted *Atlantic Monthly* Creative Writing Award, the first time that any student from Shippensburg had been so honored. When he graduated, he married his high school sweetheart, Gerda Ann Cerra, and as of this writing they are still married. Koontz went to work for the Appalachian Poverty Program for one year, a year of disillusionment in which he came to have a gut-level distrust for government schemes and programs, feeling that they are an inefficient means of getting help to those who desperately need it. He also came to feel that programs such as the Appalachian one may do more harm than good by encouraging dependency on those whose greatest need is to become independent. The distrust of government and government programs that Koontz developed then has become a common theme in his writing, and is the motivator for the many layers of action in his most complex novel, *Dark Rivers of the Heart* (1994—see Chapter 10).

After leaving the Appalachian Poverty Program, Koontz taught high school for two years while continuing to work at his own writing. Amazingly, he had sold three paperback novels and some twenty short stories by the end of this period, at which time Gerda offered to support them for five years so that Dean could pursue writing as a full-time career. Since then, he has always worked as a full-time writer, although it was about fifteen years before he could actually support both Gerda and himself through his writing, and another five years before he believed that being able to do so was something that would last. Today, he considers the writer "Dean Koontz" to be a partnership between Gerda and himself, one in which he does the writing and she handles the business aspects.

In terms of his writing schedule, Dean Koontz is one of the hardest working of contemporary authors. He spends about ten hours a day, six days a week, at his writing and this has not changed over time; if anything, he now works longer hours than he did as a beginning writer. He feels that such extended stints give him greater empathy for his characters, and clearly they reflect the fact that Dean Koontz is a writer who loves to write.

DEVELOPMENT AS A WRITER

Koontz's first novel, *Star Quest*, was published in 1968. It is also his first science fiction novel, the genre in which he worked for the next four years. At the end of that time, he wanted to branch out and try other genres, explore other modes of fiction, and in doing so, extend the possibilities available to him as a writer. Because of this, he began what was to be a fifteen-year use of various pseudonyms or pen names, so that he could do different types of writing under different names.

It is one of the realities of the publishing world that publishers are resistant to having popular writers write under the same name in more than one genre. The general belief is that audiences identify a particular author with a particular type of book, and they will be very disappointed if they buy a book written by author X, who has in the past written only adventure stories, and discover that what they have bought this time is not an adventure story but instead is a historical romance. It is also much easier to market a writer who writes only one kind of book; all the publisher has to do is say something like "Another tale of high adventure from X!" Readers know exactly what to expect and even where to find the book in a bookstore. And it is not just little-known writers who are faced with this problem. One of the world's most honored contemporary mystery writers, British author P. D. James, recently wrote a science fiction novel after having made her reputation as a writer of mysteries. Anyone who wanted to find her science fiction novel had to go to the mystery section of the bookstore, although some enlightened bookstores carried it on both their mystery and science fiction shelves.

Authors respond to such generic constraints by pointing out that if readers enjoy X's adventure stories, the chances are excellent that they'll want to read X's historical romances, too—it is the writer they enjoy rather than the genre label. Authors also say that in terms of marketing, young writers receive almost no advertising exposure from their publishers, so little is lost by a publisher not being able to use an all-purpose slogan for a given author's work. Finally, authors make the excellent point that for writers to grow in their craft they must branch out, try new things, imagine new kinds of stories.

It was in order to be able to do this kind of experimenting that in 1971, Koontz adopted his first pseudonym, Deanna Dwyer, adding to it over the years the names K. R. Dwyer, Brian Coffey, Anthony North, John Hill, Aaron Wolfe, David Axton, Leigh Nichols, Owen West, and Richard Paige. He used the Deanna Dwyer name for gothic romances, K. R. Dwyer for suspense, Brian Coffee for short suspense, Anthony North for the technothriller, John Hill for occult mystery, Aaron Wolfe for science fiction, David Axton for adventure, Leigh Nichols for romantic suspense, Owen West for horror novels, and Richard Paige for romantic suspense. By using these different names Koontz achieved his goal of being able to write—and publish—in different genres. However, he has also made it difficult for critics to track his work. Thus, Karen Springen, writing in *Newsweek*, says that Koontz has written under eight pseudonyms, *Contemporary Authors* credits him with nine pseudonyms, and *The Dean Koontz Companion* (Greenberg, Gorman, and Munster 1994) lists ten pseudonyms.

In retrospect, it would have been much easier on his readers and critics if Koontz's publishers had listened to him and allowed him to write under his own name in whatever genre he chose. It would also have made it a lot easier to determine exactly how many books Koontz has written. His publisher neatly evades the issue by saying, in an information sheet on Dean Koontz that was used to publicize *Dark Rivers of the Heart*, "Koontz has written nearly 50 books," although how near is left to the reader to determine; I make the total count to be sixty, but Jay Rosen, in a review of *Dark Rivers* in the *New York Times Book Review*, calls it Koontz's twenty-fourth book. His most recent novel, *Intensity*, would therefore be book number twenty-five rather than sixty. This raises the question of whether to count as Dean Koontz novels all the novels he has written, including those for which he used pseudonyms, or only those novels published under his own name (this seems to be how the *New York Times* has arrived at its number). If, for simplicity's sake, we follow the lead of the *New York Times*, how will reissues be counted? This is no frivolous question, since although most of Koontz' pseudonymous works are now out of print, some are slowly returning under his own name, and others he plans to revise and reissue, again using his own name. *Publishers Weekly* says, "Once Dean Koontz' writing career lifted off, he realized that as the years went by, certain of his earlier books could be sold for republication—and do better the second time around. In some cases, rather than wait for the rights to revert, he bought them back from the original publishers" (Nathan 1995, 18).

Readers interested in finding reissued Dean Koontz works should look at the copyright page of any book now in bookstores under the "Dean Koontz" name to determine whether the book is a reissue. For example, *The Face of Fear*, published as a Berkley paperback in 1985 under Koontz's name, was originally published in hardcover by Bobbs-Merrill in 1977 under the name Brian Coffey, while *The House of Thunder*, published as a Berkley paperback in 1992 under Koontz's name, was originally published as a Pocket Books paperback in 1982 under the name Leigh Nichols.

The novels that are studied in this *Critical Companion* were all originally published under the Dean Koontz name. They span the years 1976 to 1995, and include some of his writing in the horror and science fiction genres, although the overall emphasis is on what Koontz refers to as his "cross-genre" works; these cross-genre novels, which incorporate elements not only of horror and science fiction but also of the mystery, the romance, and the thriller, begin with 1980's *Whispers*. They are representative of Koontz's mature work at its best, and together the sixteen novels reflect the interests, concerns, and overall shape of his writing today. They are also books that are relatively easy for readers to find in bookstores and libraries; this, too, was a consideration in their choice. However, serious fans of Koontz's work will find it worth their time to seek out the pseudonymous works that have been reissued under the Koontz name. It will also be interesting, when Koontz begins to reissue earlier works that he has subsequently revised, to compare the originals to the revisions and, in that way, gain a sense of his development as a writer.

EMERGENCE AS A SERIOUS WRITER

Although Koontz's first novel was published in 1968, he himself marks the beginning of his career as a serious writer with the 1972 novel *Chase*, the well-reviewed story of a Vietnam veteran returned to civilian life. For the next eight years Koontz experimented with different genres and then in 1980, with the publication of *Whispers*, he had both his first paperback best-seller and his first cross-genre work. In 1986, the novel *Strangers* (see Chapter 4) became his first hardcover best-seller. With the success of this work, he was finally able to drop his use of pseudonyms and write only under his own name. He could do this because with the works that followed *Whispers*—1983's *Phantoms* (see Chapter 3), 1984's *Darkfall* (see Chapter 7), and 1986's *Strangers*—Dean Koontz succeeded in doing what he had set out to do: he created an audience for his cross-genre works or, to put it another way, he created an audience for books by Dean Koontz, whatever their genre might be. He says that now many new authors are urged by their publishers to write Dean Koontz cross-genre–type books. Maybe one day, readers will be able to find such a category neatly lined up in libraries and bookstores, perhaps between the mystery and science fiction sections.

GOALS

A goal that Dean Koontz set out to accomplish in his writing is one that can best be termed that of delivering a message. Having survived a terrifying childhood, he says, "I've written so often about people who have a disability that is tied to their past. . . . They were raised in a house where Dad was psychotic, where they had no control—and they had to endure. I've always been attracted to stories like that" (Feeney 1994, 142). As grim as this sounds, Koontz nonetheless writes books that are opti-mistic in their overall worldview—books that emphasize that while we cannot control the forces that the world will bring to bear on us, we can ultimately control how we will react to those forces. For himself, he chose to escape to the world of the imagination, and in doing so, he now creates imaginative worlds for others to escape to—worlds in which they have models of people overcoming backgrounds of abuse and terror and going on to create their own happiness. In fact, one of the reasons Koontz does not consider himself to be a writer of horror fiction is because of the underlying message in his works. In comparing himself to Stephen King, Koontz has said, "He pretty much embraces the horror label, and I don't." Interviewer Karen Springen adds, "Certainly Koontz' books are filled with dark forces and death. But unlike King, he is bullish on life; his novels invariably close with happily-ever-after-endings" (1991, 62), endings that reflect the life Koontz has created for himself, through both his enduring marriage and the joy he takes in his work. In a memorable image of him working at home, Feeney and Gleick say, "The walls of his upstairs office are lined with thousands of Koontz originals: one copy of each novel in each language in which it has been published. 'Whenever I get depressed,' the author says cheerfully, 'I stand close to these' " (1994, 142).

A NOTE ON SOURCES

Karen Springen says Dean Koontz, "is undoubtedly the least-known best-selling author in America" (1991, 62) and in fact, it is difficult to find information on him. There just isn't very much that has been written about him, perhaps because among other things his intense, sixty- to seventy-hour-a-week work schedule leaves him little time for interviews, talk-show appearances, and the like. By far the best source of information on Koontz is *The Dean Koontz Companion*, edited by Martin H. Greenberg, Ed Gorman, and Bill Munster. This 300-page work includes a lengthy interview with Koontz and an annotated bibliography of his work. It is an essential resource for anyone wishing to know about Dean Koontz as a person and as a writer. I have relied on it for much of the information included in this chapter.

CHRONOLOGY OF EVENTS

1945	July 9, 1945: Dean Ray Koontz born to Ray and Florence Koontz, Everett, Pa.
1966	Graduated from Shippensburg State College, English major, communications minor.
	Married to Gerda Ann Cerra.
	Atlantic Monthly Creative Writing Award for short story "Kittens."
1966–1967	Teacher-Counsellor, Appalachian Poverty Program.
1967–1969	English Teacher, Mechanicsburg High School.
1968	Publication of first novel, *Star Quest*.
1969	Death of Florence Koontz.
1971	Hugo Award nomination for novella *Beastchild*.
	First use of Deanna Dwyer pseudonym.

1972	Publication of *Chase*, novel Koontz considers beginning of his career as a serious writer.
	First use of K. R. Dwyer pseudonym.
1973	First use of Brian Coffey pseudonym.
1974	First use of Anthony North pseudonym.
1975	Moves to West Coast.
	First use of John Hill pseudonym.
	First use of Aaron Wolfe pseudonym.
1976	First use of David Axton pseudonym.
1979	First use of Leigh Nichols pseudonym.
1980	First paperback best-seller, *Whispers*.
	First of Koontz's cross-genre novels, *Whispers*.
	First use of Owen West pseudonym.
1985	First use of Richard Paige pseudonym.
1986	First hardcover best-seller, *Strangers*.
	End of use of pseudonyms.
1990	Death of Ray Koontz.

Genre

OVERVIEW

The word *genre* means "class" or "type," and when it is applied to literature, it refers to a particular kind of literature, such as fiction, poetry, or drama. Within each of these kinds of literature, the term is also used to designate other categories or subsets, so that the genre of fiction has within it such genres as the novel and the short story; in turn, within the genre of the novel are the different types of novels, which are further broken down into their genres. Thus, science fiction is a genre of the novel, which is in turn a genre of fiction, which is in turn a genre of literature. The genre of science fiction has within it the genres of hard science fiction, space opera, science fantasy, and so on. In other words, the term genre is simply a way of labeling literature so that people can have a frame of reference for talking about it with one another, publishers can have a way of marketing books, and librarians and bookstore owners can have a way of organizing books so that readers can easily find them.

One of the methods of dividing fiction into genres is to break it into popular fiction and mainstream fiction. While these two categories have much in common, one of their major differences is that popular fiction is written for a mass audience, whereas mainstream fiction often must create its own audience—it has no ready-made set of readers out there waiting for it. Another major difference is that popular fiction is a comforting fiction in that it reinforces our preconceptions of what people are like and how the world works, whereas mainstream fiction unsettles us by forcing us to question our preconceptions. Thus, we might come away from a mystery reassured that there are answers to questions, that the truth will out, and that the guilty will be punished. In contrast, we might come away from a work of mainstream fiction with our questions unanswered, the truth never discovered, and the guilty never identified. An underlying message to virtually all popular literature is that if one perseveres, things will work out; an underlying message to virtually all mainstream literature is that we have no choice but to persevere in the face of the fact that things may never work out.

There are fashions in literature just as there are fashions in everything. At the moment, in contemporary American culture, mainstream literature is generally held to be superior to popular literature because its worldview is considered to be more intellectually challenging. The underlying assumption here is that to be intellectually challenged is superior to being entertained. This is, of course, a value judgment, one that takes a narrow view of the possibilities of stories. All stories have the capacity to enrich our lives, whether by affirming what we believe or by causing us to question those beliefs. For this reason, each separate kind of work should be considered in the context of its own genre. It is pointless to fault a particular genre on the basis that it could or should be a different one; we can only judge works in the context of what they are.

As to what sort of books Dean Koontz writes, most critics consider him a writer of popular fiction because of his basic worldview. In nearly all of his work, his underlying message is that human beings have the capacity to create their own happiness—that while we may not be able to choose our fates, we can choose how we respond to those fates and, indeed, we have a responsibility to make such a choice. This is an optimistic outlook, one that tells us that life is what we make of it, that it is in our hands.

While there is no disagreement about the general category Koontz falls into, matters become more difficult when one tries to decide exactly which of the genres of popular fiction is represented by his work. Popular literature includes many genres, such as the Western, the thriller or suspense novel, the romance, science fiction, fantasy, horror, and mystery and detective fiction. At one time or another, Dean Koontz has written works in all of these categories except the Western, but typically his work bridges genres, containing elements of two, three, or more literary types within a single novel. He has said of his work that while he began as a writer of science fiction—since that was the fiction that he read and loved when he was growing up and, therefore, the fiction he knew best when he began to write—he has written himself out in that genre. He considers his writing today to be cross-genre, saying of the many generic elements he makes use of,

> SF is in part a fiction of ideas, so I took that aspect of the genre for my blend. From horror I borrowed mood more than anything—that cold sense of foreboding eeriness, ineffable but frightening presences at the periphery of vision, which is always a part of good horror writing. From the suspense genre I took a contemporary setting . . . as well as headlong pace and tension; few SF novels and fewer horror novels are tense and swift-moving, so I felt that I'd really have something if I coupled SF's ideas with horror's mood in a story with a suspense novel's taut pace. (Wiater 1989, 36)

Nonetheless, despite Koontz's use of a mixture of popular genres, he is most often identified as a writer of horror fiction, a label that Greenberg et al. attribute to the success of Koontz's novel *Phantoms* (see Chapter 3), which they describe as "the closest thing he has ever written to a genuine horror novel" (1994, 300). *Phantoms* was followed one year later by *Darkfall*, another classic horror novel, and it seems to be from these two works that Koontz's classification as a horror novelist comes.

HORROR

The horror genre is a mix of popular genres. It originates with the gothic novel, which gave birth to both the ghost story and the horror story. J. A. Cuddon describes the gothic as being a tale "intended to chill the spine and curdle the blood" (1991, 381), and in virtual unanimity with other critics, considers the first of the type to be Horace Walpole's *The Castle of Otranto* (1764), a work that features as its setting "a medieval castle with long underground passages, trap doors, dark stairways, and mysterious rooms whose doors slam unexpectedly" (Holman and Harmon 1992, 217). While the modern horror novel rarely takes place in such a traditional setting, one that has become a cliché of the form, it inherits from the gothic novel the goal of creating "the same atmosphere of brooding and unknown terror" (Holman and Harmon 1992, 219), and it often relies heavily on setting to contribute to this atmosphere. A fine example of this use of gothic setting is Koontz's novel *Whispers* (see Chapter 8), with its isolated house and separate, underground cellar filled with softly rustling cockroaches. An equally good example is *Cold Fire* (see Chapter 7), with creatures that bulge out of the walls in a deserted, cobweb-strewn mill and a 10,000-year-old creature living at the bottom of the mill pond.

For Cuddon, the horror story is, like the work of Dean Koontz, a broad, inclusive genre that deals with "murder, suicide, torture, fear and madness," as well as "ghosts, vampires, *doppelgangers* [i.e., doubles] succubae, incubi, poltergeists, demonic pacts, diabolic possession and exorcism, witchcraft, spiritualism, voodoo, lycanthropy [i.e, imagining oneself to be an animal such as a wolf] and the macabre" (1991, 417). He also includes telekinesis. On the basis of this description, it becomes clear why Koontz is considered to be a writer of horror fiction. Like the genre as a whole, his work is broad and inclusive, and almost every plot element listed by Cuddon can be found in his work: *Midnight* (see Chapter 7) begins with a murder disguised as a suicide; *Whispers* is centered on fear and madness and has a fine example of the *doppelganger* in its identical twins, both named Bruno; *The Bad Place* (see Chapter 8) has a quasi-vampire in the antagonist Candy; Jim Ironheart of *Cold Fire* is a poltergeist; and *Hideaway*'s Jeremy Nyebern (see Chapter 3) has made a pact with Satan, who possesses him. Voodoo is a central element in *Darkfall* (see Chapter 7), with its creatures called up from hell by a master of the black arts, and the people of *Midnight*, who turn into primitive, feral creatures, are fine examples of lycanthropy—if they are not wolves, they are certainly cousins to the wolf.

Finally, any discussion of Dean Koontz as a writer of horror fiction is inaccurate unless it emphasizes that in most of Koontz's work, horror is based on the inhumanity of one human being to another rather than on such stock supernatural devices as the cold, dismembered hand reaching out to touch someone, the door that mysteriously slams shut, the creature that scrabbles under the bed. Stories such as these last are fun to read, and once read, they are comforting because ultimately, they bring us the message that our terrors are not real, that they are just scary stories. But there is nothing comforting about Dean Koontz's descriptions of the horrors we can and do inflict on each other, and it is for this reason that many of Dean Koontz's works stay in the mind long after they have been read: his fictional horrors can be all too real, and although he insists that we can overcome them, only some of his characters—the ones we identify with—ultimately succeed in doing so.

SCIENCE FICTION

In many ways, the development of Dean Koontz's work parallels the development of the gothic novel. Where Koontz begins with science fiction; moves to horror; adds elements of the mystery, the romance, and suspense; and culminates in the technothriller, the gothic novel begins with tales of madness and terror and in turn becomes the ancestor not only of horror fiction but also of science fiction. Mary Shelley's classic gothic novel *Frankenstein* (1818), a tale of the botched scientific creation of life, is certainly a story of horror, but it is also considered by critics such as Brian Aldiss to be the first science fiction story, showing how closely these popular genres are related to one another. Aldiss defines science fiction as a fiction that focuses on "the search for a definition of mankind and his status in the universe which will stand in our advanced but confused state of knowledge (science), and is characteristically cast in the Gothic or post-Gothic mode" (1986, 26). For Rosenburg and Herald, the defining characteristic of science fiction is the fact that it is speculative: "speculative about the potential uses of science and speculative about the potential future of mankind on this world and within this universe" (1991, 192). By convention the genre is divided into hard science fiction, based on the physical sciences of biology, chemistry, physics, and so on, and soft science fiction, based on the social sciences of sociology, anthropology, psychology, and the like.

Although Dean Koontz no longer exclusively writes as a science fiction author, much of his early reading and experience in this genre is evident in the works that he calls his suspense novels. *Night Chills* (see Chapter 8), which is based on the topic of subliminal mind control, is a classic example of the social criticism genre of science fiction, a genre in which present trends are extrapolated into the near future and their consequences vividly described, often as a warning concerning what might or will happen. *The Vision* (see Chapter 4), published one year after *Night Chills*, is also a work of science fiction, although it belongs to a different genre—that of extrasensory perception, which Rosenberg and Herald define as focusing on "the powers of precognition, telepathy, clairvoyance, telekinesis, and teleportation" (1991, 205). The novel's protagonist is a clairvoyant who, when attacked by her brother, saves herself through her command of telepathy and telekinesis. And while *Phantoms* has elements of many different genres, it has a classic alien invasion opening when a protagonist enters a town, only to find that the entire town is dead or has disappeared. *Strangers* (see Chapter 4) is another good example of an alien invasion story, with its landing of a spaceship as its motivation for all subsequent action, and *Lightning* (see Chapter 6) is built on a classic plot of science fiction, one that centers on time travel and alternative histories. The novel that many readers consider to be Koontz's best book, *Watchers* (see Chapter 5), has as one of its antagonists a monster known as The Outsider, whose sole reason for existing is to act as a killing device. Since he is genetically engineered, the novel falls squarely within the science fiction genre of hard science—in this case, biology.

MYSTERY

In the classic mystery, a serious crime has been committed, disrupting the peace and stability of the society in which it has taken place. The story then centers on locating the criminal, the source of destabilization, and in some way eliminating him or her as a threat, usually through imprisonment, execution, or suicide. The well-respected writer of horror stories, Edgar Allan Poe, is also considered to be the inventor of the mystery, and so in him the separate threads of the gothic come together. Koontz introduces many of the elements of the mystery into his work, most frequently those of the police procedural. This is a subgenre in which the police are seen as ordinary people going about the ordinary routines of their job. Neither geniuses in the Sherlock Holmes mold nor outsiders like Sam Spade, they achieve results by following day-to-day, systematic procedures. Typically, their solutions are based on teamwork and luck as much as on intuitive deduction, and they are usually seen in a positive light, as hardworking people who are underpaid and underappreciated. *Watchers* includes such a procedural element in the work of the National Security Agency (NSA) agents, as does *Darkfall*, whose two protagonists are New York City police detectives. *Mr. Murder* (see Chapter 9) has an interesting variation on this theme, with its image of a policeman who, because he understands all too well the procedures of present-day policing, will take no action for fear that he will be held personally accountable. The implication here is that we live in a society in which acting as a team is no longer a given of police work.

Other elements of the mystery can be found in *Midnight*'s classic opening of a murder that is labeled suicide and in the search for the identity of an amnesiac in *The Bad Place*. However, in the mystery such events are the central element of the story, and when they have been resolved, the story comes to an end. But in both Koontz works, the mystery is solved long before the conclusion: the puzzle serves as a plot element to keep us enthralled as the larger story plays itself out rather than acting as the heart of the story.

POPULAR ROMANCE

As with horror and science fiction, the popular romance novel is a descendant of the gothic novel, but in the sunny guise in which it appears in the work of Dean Koontz, it is difficult to see the relationship. Rosenburg and Herald define the basic theme of this genre as "true love triumphant against all odds" (1991, 143). Like Dean Koontz's use of the conventions of the mystery, the conventions of the popular romance are present in his novels, but only as a secondary element. Typically, his protagonists are either happily married or become so by the novel's end, and his books are blissfully free of that stock device of the romance novel, the misunderstanding that any normal person could resolve in ten minutes but that the romance characters take 300 pages to clear up. One marked aspect of his work is that in the world of Dean Koontz, when boy meets girl there are never any doubts or second thoughts: both know at once that they are made for one another, and they turn out to be just that. While some characters are described as having been in relationships that were unhappy or destructive, these relationships have taken place before the action of the novel, and invariably, the characters find new, happy, and productive relationships by the novel's end. It is as though Dean Koontz has an image of the world in which men and women go happily two by two, never arguing, always understanding and supporting one another. This is one of the elements that makes his work optimistic: in his world, we are not necessarily doomed to be alone and misunderstood. Some typical examples of such happy relationships can be found in *Watchers*, *Lightning*, *Mr. Murder*, *Strangers* (in which almost every major character finds or affirms true love by the end of the story), and *Dark Rivers of the Heart* (see Chapter 10).

TECHNOTHRILLER

Another strong element in Dean Koontz's cross-genre novels is that of the technothriller. Michael Seidman lists the technothriller as one of the most popular of contemporary subgenres, saying that it has "replaced straightforward spy stories in the hearts of readers" (1992, 35). In these novels, the technology itself so holds our attention that it takes on the status of a character in its own right. Seidman says "the equipment itself is often the prize [in the technothriller], and its capabilities provide the twists and action" (34). Most critics date the beginning of the genre with Tom Clancy's *The Hunt for Red October* (1984), although technothriller author Stephen Coonts places it well before this, with Edward L. Beach's 1955 novel, *Run Silent, Run Deep* (Ryan 1993, 31). Some of the best examples of Koontz's use of the conventions of this genre are *Midnight*'s focus on the computer's incredible ability to access information; the details on weapons and security measures in *Watchers*; the well-described use of surveillance and tracking equipment in *Mr. Murder*; and in one of the most recent books considered here, 1994's *Dark Rivers of the Heart*, Koontz has created a technothriller centered on the question of who will control cyberspace and, by controlling it, gain the power to control society. Descriptions of the various uses and applications of computers, especially the trapping of a Japanese satellite named *Godzilla*, are among the most gripping scenes in the novel.

In sum, then, while Dean Koontz is generally categorized as a writer of horror, this has far more to do with the fact that his early successes were in this area than it does with the many different generic conventions he uses in his work. Of course, in this he is working well within the tradition of such classic horror writers as Edgar Allan Poe, who wrote stories that would now be categorized as horror, others that would be categorized as suspense, and still others that would be categorized as mystery and detective fiction, although Poe was probably unaware of being a cross-genre author, since the concept of popular genres is a relatively late twentieth-century phenomenon.

When considering exactly which category best fits the work of Dean Koontz, of the sixteen books considered in this Critical Companion, only six—*Phantoms, Darkfall, Midnight, The Bad Place, Cold Fire,* and *Hideaway*—fit well in the horror genre, and even these frequently include elements of other genres as well. For this reason, it seems not only a courtesy to the author to categorize him as he wishes to be categorized—that is, as a writer of cross-genre works—but also the most accurate description of the kind of writing he does. And since there is, at least so far, no such category as cross-genre, his works are best described under the label of thriller or suspense, two terms that are used interchangeably. For example, *Genreflecting*, in Rosenberg and Herald's discussion of the thriller, says, "Suspense is the code word for the thriller" (Rosenberg and Herald 1991, 47). Other examples of the interchangeability of the terms thriller and suspense can be seen in the fact that in its review of *Dark Rivers of the Heart, Kirkus Reviews* called the book a thriller, whereas *Library Journal* called the same novel a suspense novel. The magazine *The Armchair Detective* reached what may be the best resolution of this issue of genre. The magazine groups its book reviews according to type, and rather than decide if a work is a thriller or a suspense novel, it combines the two labels and lists such books as Thriller/Suspense. I have chosen to use the term suspense rather than thriller as the general one for the works of Dean Koontz that are covered in this Critical Companion because, regardless of the generic conventions he uses in any one novel, all of his novels have the element of suspense as defined in *Genreflecting*: "the characters and the reader are in a constant state of uneasy anticipation of the worst, which all too often happens" (Rosenberg and Herald 1991, 47). However, I might as easily have used thriller, following Cuddon's definition of the term: "in fiction it is a tense, exciting, tautly plotted and sometimes sensational type of novel . . . in which action is swift and suspense continual." This sounds definitive, but it is prefaced by Cuddon's statement that the word *thriller* is "a vague term, perhaps no longer particularly useful for purposes of categorization" (1991, 971). Given this vagueness of meaning, I prefer instead to use Koontz's definition of himself as a cross-genre writer to describe the particular genre he fits into, and here I make the revolutionary assumption that very possibly the author knows best what kind of books he writes.

Phantoms
(1983)

It is characteristic of Dean Koontz's work to introduce certain elements in one novel and then develop them further in subsequent novels, as though they had stayed in his mind long after he was finished with the initial work and he wanted to look at them from other perspectives before letting them go. Chapter 8 discusses this pattern in terms of the novels *The Bad Place*, *Night Chills*, and *Whispers*. Another example of this is 1983's *Phantoms*, whose central theme Koontz revisits in 1992's *Hideaway*, developing in the two works two different concepts of the nature of evil.

Like nearly all Dean Koontz's later novels, *Phantoms* is a cross-genre novel that borrows conventions from several genres. It fits best in the suspense category, a broad group covering works of many genres and having as a defining characteristic the fact that "the characters and the reader are in a constant state of uneasy anticipation of the worst, which all too often happens" (Rosenberg and Herald 1991, 47). *Phantoms* opens like a classic work of science fiction, with the protagonist entering a town, only to find everyone dead. The solution to the deaths puts the novel in the subgenre of science fantasy, in which new laws of nature—laws other than those operating in our world—are at play. *Phantoms* also includes elements of the romance in the relationship between the protagonists, of the procedural in its descriptions of the way in which the chemical and biological warfare teams operate, of the mystery in terms of who is doing the killings and what that person or thing's motives are, and of the horror novel in its use of dead creatures who return as zombies, although in the denouement the horror aspect is undercut, since the supernatural aspects of the anatagonist or villain are given natural explanations.

PLOT DEVELOPMENT

A plot can usually be divided into four parts: the original situation, the complications, the crisis or climax, and the denouement. The original situation is the world of the work of fiction before something happens to disrupt it. In *Phantoms*, this situation is that Jennifer Paige, a thirty-one-year-old doctor, is on her way home to Snowfield, California, a ski resort where she lives and has her medical practice. Her fourteen-year-old sister Lisa is with her because, with the death of their mother six weeks earlier, Jennifer is Lisa's guardian (their father died many years before the story takes place). Lisa discovered her mother's body, a terrible shock for anyone, let alone a young girl, and the task before Jenny and Lisa is to create a new family in the absence of their parents. Because Jenny is so much older than Lisa and has not lived at home with her since Lisa was two, they are in the process of feeling out how to do this when the novel opens.

Complications are something out of the ordinary, something that the characters must deal with in some way. Often, there is an initial major complication that puts into play a whole series of further complications. In *Phantoms* the initial complication is the sense that something is wrong, something is out of the ordinary in Snowfield. When Jenny and Lisa arrive, everything is very quiet—too quiet. There are no people on the streets and no one can be seen at the windows of any of the houses or shops, even though there are lights on in all of these places and the town looks as it usually does. At Jenny's house, no one answers when she enters and calls out that she is home. Where is her housekeeper? This question is quickly answered when Jenny goes into the kitchen and finds the housekeeper lying on the floor in front of the sink, dead. The death brings about further complications, since it appears that the housekeeper is uniformally bruised on every surface of her body, and this is the only sign of the cause of death: there is no blood, no wound, no sign of struggle. As a doctor, Jenny knows of nothing that could cause such a death. When she tries to use the telephone to report finding the body, she cannot get a dial tone, although the line seems open and she has a sense of someone lurking on it, listening to her. Jenny goes to her next door neighbor's house to make the call, but there is no one there, even though dinner is on the table and, from all appearances, the family had just started eating.

The scene then shifts to the county sheriff's station, where Sheriff Bryce Hammond is questioning Fletcher Kale, who is suspected of killing his wife and son. Through his questioning it becomes obvious that Hammond, who gives the initial impression of being a country bumpkin, is a very sharp policeman and no one's fool. As a result of Hammond's probing interrogation Kale falls apart, and it is clear that he will be charged with the murders. This scene also provides background on Hammond, whose wife died a year ago when her car was hit by a drunk driver, and whose seven-year-old son has been in a coma ever since. Hammond has been in despair, and is only beginning to come out of it as the novel opens.

In Snowfield, Jenny finally gets a dial tone and is able to get through to the sheriff's station. She reports that something is terribly wrong in the town, maybe a lethal epidemic, maybe something else, but whatever it is, the entire town of five hundred people seems to be dead, one huge morgue. Hammond goes to Snowfield with five of his men and they search the town, finding such appalling things as severed heads in the ovens at the local bakery and severed hands clutching a rolling pin. As they investigate, the characters feel as though something in the town is watching their every move, and they are proved right. One by one, the sheriff's men are picked off, with the first victim, a deputy noted for his caution, disappearing into thin air. Apparently, caution is no defense against whatever is in Snowfield. The second victim, another deputy, does not disappear, but instead is attacked by a giant pterodactyl-like moth, who sucks off his face and even the brain from out of his skull. This victim had been saying that all the other characters were being too imaginative, that everything could be rationally explained, that there was nothing weird going on in Snowfield. Clearly, denial is no more of a defense than was caution.

A message is found written in eyebrow pencil on a bathroom mirror saying, "Timothy Flyte, The Ancient Enemy." Two victims, also completely covered with bruises, are in the bathroom, having apparently locked themselves in there shortly before being killed. Does this mean that Timothy Flyte has caused the deaths and disappearances? If so, who is Timothy Flyte? At this point, a series of very strange phenomena are documented. The characters notice that there are no animals left in town, and that while they are finding some bodies, they aren't finding nearly as many as they should: most of the townspeople seem to have disappeared, leaving no physical trace behind them. Weird voices, perhaps those of the people and animals who were taken away, come over the telephone lines. In terms of a probable cause, the characters now begin to wonder if some sort of secret biological or chemical warfare agent could have been released in Snowfield. Sheriff Hammond, who is an old friend of the governor's, calls him and gets his permission to bring in the Chemical and Biological Warfare Defense Unit from Dugway, Utah. This team enters the town and establishes that whatever is going on in Snowfield, it is not chemical, not biological, and not an alien, extraterrestrial creature.

The setting now switches to London, where Timothy Flyte, an old man, is being taken to lunch by his American publisher. Many years earlier Flyte wrote a book on unexplained disappearances in history, such as that of the Roanoke colony in Virginia and, later, the disappearance of the ship *Mary Celeste*, with all of her crew. In his book, *The Ancient Enemy*, Flyte speculated that the cause of these disappearances was a being he called The Ancient Enemy, a prehistoric creature who from time to time preys on humans and animals, although It does most of its preying in the oceans, which is why humans have so little knowledge of It. The Ancient Enemy can be known only by its actions, rather than by eye-witness reports, since It usually operates where no one can see It and in the rare cases where It attacks people, no one is left alive to report the attack. Flyte's book is long out of print, a collector's item, and Flyte himself lost his teaching position as a result of writing the book, which was considered to be radical and unscientific, not to say bizarre, by his university colleagues. Flyte's American publisher now wants Flyte to write a popularization of his book for a mass audience.

The scene then shifts back to Snowfield, where the Chemical and Biological Warfare (CBW) team is performing autopsies, running lab tests, and the like—and in the process, being picked off one by one by whatever it is that is causing the deaths and disappearances in the town. The team establishes that the cause of death is some sort of living creature, but it does so at great cost to itself: only one of the CBW team is left after the initial investigations, Sara Yamaguchi, a geneticist. At this point, whatever is killing everyone and everything in Snowfield begins communicating to the survivors by computer, taunting them with hints as to who and what It is. It requests the presence of Timothy Flyte, whom

It refers to as its biographer, promising him safe passage if he will come to Snowfield.

While this is happening, Fletcher Kale, the accused wife and child murderer, escapes from prison, kills a deputy, and flees to a mountain retreat on the other side of Snowfield. At the same time, a motorcycle gang has gone to this hideaway, with neither Kale nor the motorcyclists knowing that the other is there. Thus, Sheriff Hammond, his two surviving deputies, and Jenny, Lisa, and Sara are in Snowfield, with Fletcher Kale and a motorcycle gang very nearby; It, the creature responsible for all the devastation, is seemingly everywhere in the area. Before Kale reaches the retreat, It has picked off most of the motorcycle gang and only its leader, Gene Terr, is left to greet him, deep inside a limestone cavern.

The focus switches back to Snowfield and the arrival of Timothy Flyte, who explains to the sheriff's crew and the other survivors that, in his view, It is The Ancient Enemy, a creature that has existed for eons and may have been responsible for the disappearance of the dinosaurs as well as of all the living creatures in the town. When Flyte communicates via computer with It, the creature reveals itself as an egocentric monster who wants Flyte to write about and celebrate what It is, since it is Flyte who first recognized the being's true nature. Flyte accuses It of having a human ego and says that It owes human beings for its intelligence. He maintains that, as It has absorbed humans and animals, so too has It absorbed their intelligence and ego. But It will have none of this, and continues to see itself as far superior to human beings.

While Flyte and The Ancient Enemy are communicating, Sara Yamaguchi discovers through her tests that the creature is chemically similar to petrolatum, and she hypothesizes that perhaps It can be destroyed by the bacteria that is used to eat oil spills. She calls for the necessary equipment to attempt this, under the guise of doing yet further tests to learn about and celebrate the fabulous It, and she turns out to be right: the creature can indeed by destroyed in this way.

Yamaguchi's discovery leads to the climax, which is both the turning point and the emotional high point of the story. This is a very dramatic scene, with the survivors spraying the creature with the bacteria and the creature attempting to kill the surviviors in retaliation. It succeeds in killing one of the deputies and Sara Yamaguchi, and in wounding a second deputy before succumbing to the spray and, like the townspeople, disappearing. It returns to its temporary base in the limestone caverns, where Kale and Terr are worshipping It as Satan. Telling them that its time is not yet come but that It will return, It gives them five commands to carry out, promising them that if they do so, they will have immortality and then It slowly disappears.

Finally, the denouement presents the consequence or consequences of the action that has occurred in the climax and acts as a wrapping up of the story. In *Phantoms*, the denouement takes place at the hospital in nearby Santa Mira, where Jenny and Lisa are visiting the surviving deputy, who is being treated for his injuries and is already nearly recovered. By coincidence, Sheriff Hammond is also at the hosptial, visiting his son, and at this moment Gene Terr and Fletcher Kale burst in with guns at the ready, following out the creature's five commands: kill all five of these people. Hammond kills Kale and the deputy kills Terr, both of whom are very surprised to be mortal after all. Time then jumps forward and we learn that the surviving deputy will probably find happiness with a nurse he met in the hospital, that Lisa has come to terms with her mother's death and is now living a normal teenager's life, that the sheriff and Jenny are married, and that he has had what may be a prophetic dream in which he has seen his son coming out of his coma. In other words, all of the survivors have achieved a happy ending.

CHARACTER DEVELOPMENT

As a general rule, Dean Koontz's characters tend to be flat (one-dimensional) and static (nonchanging), since his plots are usually incident-driven rather than character-driven. That is the case with *Phantoms*, where only the major characters can be said to have any development, and even this is limited.

There are a group of protagonists in the novel, led by Sheriff Bryce Hammond. He is one of the few characters who can be described as round, or well developed, since we know of the tragedy that has occurred in his family and of his consequent state of mind. He is also shown, in the context of his work, in an interrogation scene that gives him stature as a hero by showing how, through adept questioning, he traps a murderer who might otherwise have gotten away with his crime. Clearly, Hammond is an intelligent, astute man. Later, in Snowfield, we see that his men hold him in high regard, again attesting to his qualities as a keeper of the law. When he leaps into a pit to spray the creature who has devastated the town, he shows great physical courage. If it is Sara Yamaguchi who works out how to kill the creature, it is Bryce Hammond who actually performs the deed. He is also a dynamic character since he changes over the course of the novel, from a man who lives in bleak despair to a man who now has hope, who believes that there is meaning to everything that happens in life.

The second major protagonist is Jennifer Paige, who is the first to discover what has happened in Snowfield. A doctor who went through medical school on scholarships, she is obviously intelligent, knowledgeable about many things such as how to handle weapons, and immensely brave. She examines the bodies of the dead even when she and her sister Lisa are the only living people in Snowfield, and she stands up to and intimidates the leader of the motorcycle gang in a fine scene in which, as she tells Hammond, she first pulls a gun on him and then explains to him quietly that she is a doctor and that *"he* might need a doctor some day. What if he took a spill off that bike of his and was lying on the road, critically injured, and *I* was the doctor who showed up—after he'd hurt me and given me good reason to hurt him in return? I told him there are things a doctor can do to complicate injuries, to make sure the patient has a long and painful recovery. I asked him to think about that'' (119).

Like Bryce Hammond, Jenny is also a round character, since we have information on who she is and on how she came to be that way. She has been in an abusive relationship with a lover, and breaking out of it was the catalyst that gave her the strength to become a doctor and make an independent life for herself. She is, however, a static character, since this significant change took place long before *Phantoms* begins. In *Phantoms*, she does gain a certain amount of insight into her mother and the mother's attitudes toward her, but other than this, she remains at the end the same brave, resourceful woman she was at the beginning. The other two women characters, Sara Yamaguchi and Lisa Paige, Jenny's younger sister, are flat and static. Sara is bright, brave, and resourceful—characteristics that remain the same throughout the novel—and that is all the information given about her. Lisa is also brave, worships her older sister, and has had a hard time coming to terms with her mother's death. Her only dynamic characteristic is in a scene at the end of the novel, where she participates in conversation and socializing and clearly enjoys herself. This is a new response for Lisa, signifying that sufficient time has passed for her to accept the death, and she is now getting on with her life. Other than this, she acts primarily as a foil to her sister, giving us a sense of Jenny from someone other than Jenny herself.

The remaining protaganists are the CBW team, a group that is killed off so quickly most readers will have trouble even remembering their names, and Sheriff Bryce Hammond's deputies, who with one exception are each given a single identifying characteristic to differentiate them one from another and who remain static throughout the novel, right up until the moment when the creature takes them. The exception is Tal Whitman, one of Koontz's many positively drawn African-American characters. We are given his background in New York City's Harlem, and like Jenny, it is his reaction to the adversity he experienced there that has made him the strong person he is today. He is the only deputy who survives the encounter with the creature, and there is some indication that he, too, is a dynamic character. In Snowfield he has learned to acknowledge fear rather than to deny it, and this acknowledgment seems to have opened him to the possibility of a romance with his hospital nurse at the end of the novel.

A final positive character is Timothy Flyte, the author of *The Ancient Enemy* and the only one to understand what the creature is and what motivates it. He is drawn as a stock character—that is, a flat character who has become a convention in certain forms of literature, such as the hard-boiled detective, the wicked witch, or the cruel stepmother. Flyte is the stereotypical scientist, the intellectual who lives for his theories and has little or no sense of reality outside of them, and this concept of him fits well with the brief appearance he makes in the novel. He is also a static character, since he too remains the same throughout the work, although he does have the satisfaction of seeing his theories proven correct. However, since he dies immediately thereafter, there is no possibility for any significant change to take place.

Phantoms has three antagonists, or villains: the murderer Fletcher Kale, the biker leader Gene Terr, and the creature that Flyte names The Ancient Enemy. Considering the small part that he plays in the novel, Kale is both round and dynamic. His psychology is drawn in more detail than that of any character, with the sheriff deciding that even though he doesn't think Kale is quite a sociopath or psychopath,

> a good cop would recognize the type and see the potential for criminal activity and, perhaps, the talent for brute violence, as well. There is a certain kind of man who has a lot of vitality and likes plenty of action, a man who has more than his share of shallow charm, whose clothes are more expensive than he can afford, who owns not a single book . . . who seems to have no well-thought-out opinions about politics or art or

economics or any issue of real substance, who is not religious except when misfortune befalls him or when he wishes to impress someone with his piety . . . who has an athletic build but who seems to loathe any pursuit as healthy as physical exercise, who spends his leisure time in bars and cocktail lounges, who cheats on his wife as a matter of habit . . . who is impulsive, who is unreliable and always late for appointments . . . whose goals are either vague or unrealistic . . . who frequently overdraws his checking account and lies about money, who is quick to borrow and slow to pay back, who exaggerates, who *knows* he's going to be rich one day but who has no specific plan for acquiring that wealth, who never doubts or thinks about next year, who worries only about himself and only when it's too late. (60)

This is a great deal of background on a character who appears in only a handful of brief scenes in the novel, and it is possible that Kale is as richly conceived as he is because he is based on Koontz's abusive father, Ray Koontz. There is certainly a marked similarity between Kale and the father, as his son Dean has described him in interviews (see Chapter 1).

In addition to being a round character Fletcher Kale is also dynamic, since even though his appearances are brief, he comes to understand that he thoroughly enjoyed murdering his wife and child, that he is committed to evil, and that he worships Satan—insights that he did not have at the beginning of the story.

Like the protagonist Timothy Flyte, the biker Gene Terr is a stock character, in this case a motorcycle gang member. Terr drinks, does dope, rapes women, and is a killer. His men worship him. He is every really bad Hell's Angels rider rolled into one, and unlike Kale, he does not change during the novel. He has always known that he is a creature of Satan and he revels in doing evil acts. The only possibility for change in Terr occurs so close to his death that he never has the chance to gain any insight from it, and this is the death itself. He had been promised by The Ancient Enemy that he would be immortal, but by the time he discovers that he is not, it's too late—he dies immediately afterward.

Fletcher Kale and Gene Terr are not inhabitants of the town, nor are they members of any group seeking to contain the monster, and the brief interactions they have with other characters are peripheral to the main story. Yet each is carefully drawn, given descriptions that contain a great amount of detail for such minor figures. This suggests that the characters are not minor, that there is something about them that is significant to the novel as a whole. In examining the effect that each has on the novel, the reader can see that they add stature to the protagonists. It is Sheriff Bryce Hammond's questioning of Fletcher Kale that shows the reader how very intelligent and insightful Hammond is, and it is Jenny Paige's facing down of Gene Terr that shows her bravery and resourcefulness. However, these are the only interactions that Kale and Terr have with other characters in the novel until almost the last scene, and it would be relatively easy to establish Hammond and Paige's qualities in ways that are more integral to the plot, displaying their characteristics by showing how they respond to the situation in Snowfield—something that Koontz does anyway.

Kale and Terr also interact with the creature itself, and they are the only characters who can be said to have a positive reaction to It. The creature does not threaten them, does not eat away at them, does not absorb them into itself or cause them to disappear, as It has with everyone else It comes across. Instead, Terr tells Kale that the creature listens to his secrets and approves of him. Terr's secrets consist of the fact that he and his gang routinely abducted young women, raped them, and then killed them in horribly drawn-out ways. The fact that the creature approves of Terr attests to the fact that the monster is pure evil, and encourages and solicits evil in others. For this reason, It is also attracted to Kale, the baby killer. It is as though Terr and Kale validate the monster and the monster in turn validates them. All celebrate the same concept, with Terr and Kale believing the creature to be Satan and the creature revelling in their belief and worship, for which they have been promised immortality. It would seem, then, that what is being developed here is the concept that evil exists absolutely, in human beings as well as in supernatural creatures.

However, the fact that Terr and Kale are killed in their final attack on the survivors causes the reader to question this interpretation and suggests a final theory of evil that is more limited and less ominous than what has been initially proposed. If Terr and Kale shed light on evil, then the light that they shed ultimately has more to do with what it shows about them than it does with what it shows about Satan. The information we have been given about them is, after all, credible: they really are murderers who delight in their acts. The information we are given about the creature is less credible, though: It promises immortality, but does not follow through. The suggestion here is that we can trust only what the characters tell us, not what the creature tells us; if we are to know the nature of evil, we can learn it only from human beings who are themselves evil, people like the doomed Terr and Kale.

The final antagonist in *Phantoms* is the creature The Ancient Enemy. While it is not a flat character, since we know a great deal about its historical background—its actions, the source of its intelligence and ego, and even what it is made up of—it is certainly a static character: it begins and ends as a source of terror, pain, and death to all living creatures.

SETTING

Dean Koontz typically uses setting as a backdrop for the action of the characters rather than as a motivating force in and of itself. Many of his novels take place in California, particularly the Laguna Seco area where he lives, and he uses such standard devices as storms to indicate that something very bad is about to happen or fog to show that characters are bewildered and do not know which way to turn. In his works the country often serves as an outpost or retreat to which characters withdraw for the safety that they hope distance and isolation will provide—and which they sometimes do provide, depending on the novel. In *Phantoms*, though, there is no safety to be found in the country. The story takes place in Snowfield, an idyllic ski resort in the California Sierras, and it is in this peaceful retreat with its alpine scenery and rustic homes that the creature makes its attack, killing everyone in the town. The actions of the creature, contrasted with the beauty and tranquillity of the town, add to the monster's fearfulness. If people cannot be safe in Snowfield, then there is nowhere on earth they can be safe.

Another good use of natural setting is the limestone cavern where the creature originally surfaces and where it retreats to die. There really are underground rivers in such caverns. These rivers do eventually lead to the sea, where The Ancient Enemy originated, and strange life-forms do live in caverns—fish and insects that never see the sun and so are white and sightless because of living in eternal darkness. If a monster really were to appear, surely it would choose a place like this, one that is already home to monsters.

The weather plays the role it usually does in Koontz's novels, acting as a portent of what is to come. Thus, when Jenny is trying to contact her neighbors, a whirlwind comes up signifying confusion, and at the climax of the novel, a heavy fog settles over the town, symbolizing the imminent coming of the creature, which like the fog can drift into any shape it chooses. And in the closing scene, the action takes place on the golden beach at Waikiki, moving from the cold mountains with their memories of death to the warm seashore with its promise of life.

Finally, Koontz makes good use of the rustic houses in Snowfield to show how vulnerable human beings are to The Ancient Enemy. Even when they have locked every window and bolted every door, It finds a way in, maybe through a keyhole, maybe through an air vent, maybe through a sink drain. Again, the message is that there is no safe place, not even one's carefully locked and shuttered home. And Koontz uses the strange decontamination suits of the Chemical and Biological Warfare team to illustrate how strange and esoteric the work is that they do. Finally, Koontz has Jenny Paige drive a Pontiac TransAm, a sleek, fast, macho car that signifies how strong, brave, and liberated Jenny is. A TransAm may not be the average doctor's car, but it does very well as the car of a woman who has the courage to face down a biker.

POINT OF VIEW

Dean Koontz's point of view—that is, the perspective from which his novels are told—is most often third-person omniscient, in which an unknown narrator can see into the minds of all the characters. This lends itself very well to his complex story lines. In *Phantoms* this point of view serves the story well because there are so many characters—the sheriff and his deputies, the CBW team members, the townspeople, the escaped murder suspect, the motorcycle gang members, the doctor and her sister, the author Flyte and his publisher. Third-person omniscient allows Koontz to give the reader significant information when it is necessary to plot development without overwhelming the reader with multiple points of view. It contributes to character development by showing inner conflicts that reach resolution at the novel's end—conflicts that the characters themselves would be unlikely to disclose, as for example the sheriff's reaction to his son's coma and Tal Whitman's experiences with fear. Another advantage to the use of third-person omniscient is that it allows Koontz to show everyone's reactions to the creature that has brought pain and death to the town; the combined weight of these reactions makes the creature that much more fearful, adding to the terror of the story.

Finally, this point of view enables Koontz to enter the mind of the creature and, in doing so, to construct a mentality that is a composite of all the minds it has absorbed. The only other possibility for such a broad point of view in *Phantoms* would be third-person limited (in which one character tells the story from the third-person point of view and the reader sees only what that character sees), with the point of view shared among many different characters. But this would be cumbersome for the reader to follow, since there are so many characters. There are just too many isolated but significant incidents involving different people to make third-person limited a practical choice, especially considering that some of these incidents are known only to the person involved and, for plot reasons, cannot be discussed. The geneticist Sara Yamaguchi, for instance, cannot explain to the other characters her plan for destroying the monster, since it is essential to the plan that it be kept secret. The monster overhears everything that goes on in the town, and if Sara were to discuss her idea with anyone, the creature would kill her before she had a chance to implement it. In contrast, the use of the omniscient point of view allows the reader to know what it is that Sara is trying to do even though none of the characters know this. It increases tension as we hold our breaths in the hope that the creature cannot read Sara's mind and that none of the others will ask questions that will make It suspicious of her requests for numerous supplies.

THEMATIC ISSUES

In *Phantoms*, the reader notices over and over the countless references to Satanic imagery and to evil as an actual and eternal entity. Characters who come into contact with the creature are struck by an overwhelming sense of evil, even when that contact is only through an open telephone line on which the creature says nothing, but just listens. When Lisa Paige looks into the eyes of one of the creature's victims, she compares it to looking into a chamber of hell. Tal Whitman, who believes that there is power in being a good, responsible person, begins to doubt that belief when he comes into contact with the creature, who seems to him to represent undefeatable evil. One of the CBW men who will be killed by the creature in a tunnel imagines the tunnel as an entrance to hell, and when he looks at the exit to the tunnel, an exit he will never reach, it looks to him like a church window; just before he dies, he specifically refers to the creature as the devil. Timothy Flyte tells his publisher that the creature, The Ancient Enemy, was identified by American Indians with their concept of Satan. The creature tells Sara Yamaguchi and Bryce Hammond that It is all the demons of hell, and lists them by name. Perhaps most terrifying of all, when the creature kills a priest in the small Catholic church in Snowfield, It does not absorb him as It has done with its other victims but instead, in a scene of absolute blasphemy, It crucifies him, nailing him to the cross over the figure of Christ. The message here seems overwhelming that The Ancient Enemy is Satan, God's fallen angel who has existed for all time and who will exist even beyond time since, like God, he is eternal.

However, in the denouement, Koontz asks the reader to reconsider this easy answer. First, there is the fact that the creature is killed. If the creature really were Satan, who in Christian doctrine is immortal, obviously it could not be killed. Also, there is Jenny Paige's speculation that if the creature has gained its intelligence from human beings, perhaps it has also gained its cruelty and viciousness from them. Maybe the creature is only a devil that human beings have created in their own image. And finally, Kale and Terr, who think of themselves as the apostles of Satan, do not succeed in carrying out the supposed Satan's tasks; instead, they themselves die, in refutation of the promise that they will be eternal. It would, therefore, seem that if there is indeed a Satan, this Ancient Enemy is not it and, further, that Satan may be nothing more than our creation. This is an optimistic concept, since it suggests that evil can at least be contained, even if it cannot be eradicated. It is, after all, much easier to control other humans and their creations than it is to control a supernatural being. The conclusion of the novel is equivocal: there may be a Satan and there may be a God, but we cannot really know this. All we can know is that life does have a purpose.

This peaceful, balanced resolution is in sharp contrast to Koontz's later exploration of the nature of evil in the novel *Hideaway*, which concludes with the message that Satan exists, that his minions are real, and that the best we can do is carry on bravely in the face of such knowledge. In this work, Lindsey and Hatch Harrison, an artist and an antiques dealer, respectively, are driving in a snow storm. Their car goes off the road and into a ravine. Lindsey frees herself and then pulls her husband out of the car, holding him in raging, freezing waters until rescue comes. (Lindsey is one of Koontz's many strong female characters.) The Harrisons are taken to a hospital, where the dead-on-arrival Hatch is brought back to life by Dr. Jonas Nyebern, a resuscitation specialist. The scene in which this is done by Nyebern and his medical team is absolutely gripping, attesting to the careful research Koontz does for each of his novels.

Hatch's return to life becomes a new beginning for him and Lindsey. Five years earlier they lost a young son to cancer and they have been grieving ever since, but now both have a new appreciation for being alive and for having one another. As a result, they adopt a child, ten-year-old Regina, a bright, witty, book-loving girl with a disability—a malformed leg and hand. Together, the three of them begin to build a family.

However, one odd side effect of the resuscitation experience is that Hatch now has bad dreams in which he seems to be in the mind of a psychopath—Jeremy Nyebern, son of the doctor who revived Hatch. When Jeremy was eighteen, he killed his mother and his sister and then committed suicide. Like Hatch, Jeremy was also revived by Dr. Nyebern, and he then escaped from the hospital and went into hiding. Jeremy believes that when he initially died he went to Hell, where he became Vassago, a crown prince of Satan. His goal now is to earn his way back there by committing crimes as horrendous as his original crimes. He therefore decides to kill Lindsey and Regina, another mother and daughter pair. He knows of them because just as Hatch can see into Jeremy's mind, so Jeremy can see into Hatch's. Jeremy and Hatch, because of their shared experience of having died and been resuscitated, share a mental bond over which they have no control.

Jeremy kidnaps Regina, and when Lindsey and Hatch follow him to rescue her, Hatch recognizes Jeremy as Vassago and tells Jeremy that he, Hatch, is Uriel, one of God's archangels. Each recognizes the other as a supernatural being and, in doing so, confirms that there is an afterlife and that it consists of a heaven and a hell, a place of good and a place of evil. Hatch then beats Jeremy to death with a crucifix and Regina is rescued. The novel concludes with a very subdued ending: Dr. Nyebern becomes a veterinarian and the other characters carry on with their lives. Lindsey still paints, Hatch sells antiques, and Regina seems well on her way to becoming a successful writer—but the tone is very low key. Dean Koontz's usual sense of the triumph of good over evil is here replaced with a sense that while evil has been defeated, the defeat has been at great cost to the characters, who will now wearily go on with lives that are not the innocent, joyful lives they might have been. Finally, Koontz's message is that evil is infinite and eternal, and that to even innocently experience evil is to be tarnished and soiled by it.

On the surface, *Hideaway*, with its focus on cutting edge, high-technology medicine, seems a far cry from *Phantoms*, a work whose plot is a classic seen over and over again in science fiction stories, novels, and movies. However, each work explores the same underlying concern: the nature of evil.

ALTERNATIVE READING:
THE AUDIENCE-CENTERED NOVEL

Readers of popular fiction—science fiction, mysteries, romances, Westerns, and the like—have definite expectations of each particular genre. Science fiction, no matter what else it does, must have some scientific concept projected into the future and developed beyond its actual contemporary practice. A mystery must have some sort of central question and that question must in some way be resolved at the novel's end. A romance must have two people in love who find resolution of their love at the conclusion. A Western must be set in some recognizable Western setting and must consider the importance of the individual as a causative agent.

Readers who choose popular fiction for their entertainment assume that their anticipations regarding a specific genre will be fulfilled, and they are willing to go some good way in cooperating with the author so that this can happen. They are basically friendly readers. They are more than willing to accept that a murder could occur in a locked room, provided the author gives them some reason—and it doesn't have to be all that plausible a reason—to accept this notion. And they are more than willing to accept that there are superior beings on other planets who come from civilizations far in advance of ours and who long to do nothing more than journey to earth and give us their wisdom. All readers ask in return for such acceptance is that the author go half-way with the reader in creating a scenario by which such benevolence on the part of alien races can be accepted, at least for the duration of the story.

Readers are willing to take part in a conspiracy with the author—to pretend that fantasy is reality—because they enjoy the genre or genres involved and because they want to be entertained. The technical term for conspiring with the author in this way is "the willing suspension of disbelief," which is defined as "the willingness [of the reader] to withhold questions about truth, accuracy, or probability in a work. This willingness to suspend doubt makes possible the temporary acceptance [by the reader] of an author's imaginative world" (Holman and Harman 1992, 464).

Every work of fiction ultimately depends on such a suspension of disbelief. After all, the reader on some level really does know that the story is only a story and that the characters are only make-believe. Nonetheless, so great is our love of stories and storytelling that we are more than willing to accept the fiction for reality, at least while we are reading the story, if only the author will give us the bare bones of plausibility that will allow us to do this—to enter the world of the author and pretend that it is the real, everyday world.

One interesting way of analyzing a work of fiction—particularly a work of popular fiction, where there are definite audience expectations— is to consider exactly how the author has gone about creating plausibility for the reader. This is especially to the point in a work like *Phantoms*. None of us in real life has ever entered a town where everyone has suddenly vanished, in the middle of meals, leaving behind only a few corpses with a cause of death that can't be determined. But Koontz makes this scenario believable to readers by reminding us of the many unexplained disappearances that have actually occurred. Where *did* the dinosaurs go, and what *did* happen to the colony at Roanoke, Virginia, and why *can't* we find any trace of the aviator Amelia Earhart, and how *about* those ships at sea that just disappear with all their crew members and never even send out a radio signal? If all of these things have happened, and we know that they have, since they are referred to in our history books and at the end of the novel the author documents them for us in a final note to the reader, then surely we can accept, at least for the duration of 400 pages, that the people of an entire (although small) town could disappear. And if we find it hard to believe that bacteria of some sort could just eat up the creature who has so terrorized the town, the same end note assures that there really are such patented microorganisms, although they are too fragile to survive outside of the laboratory.

Another way that Koontz creates plausibility is by anticipating a reader's likely objections. For example, when the first deputy disappears from the midst of the sheriff's group in Snowfield, the reader might well think, "Hey, wait a minute. Why just take one of them? Why not all of them?" But before this question can get in the way of reader enjoyment, Koontz has one of the characters ask the same question. As a possible answer, Jenny Paige speculates that the creature is teasing with them, playing with them in the same way that a cat plays with a mouse. The characters all accept this explanation, paving the way for the reader to accept it, too. Later in the novel, when Stu Wargle, the creature's second victim, is maintaining that there is nothing unusual about what's going on, that everybody is just imagining things, the reader is persuaded to put no faith at all in his interpretation because he is the one negative character in the group, a man too stupid and unimaginative to believe the evidence of his own eyes. Since the reader certainly does not want to identify with Wargle, the reader distrusts his perceptions and is therefore biased to accept that the creature is as weird as the other characters find it to be.

And as to why people haven't seen the creature before now if it has existed for so long, Flyte tells us that there are probably very, very few of these beings and that they probably live deep in ocean trenches, hibernating for years and eating mainly off ocean creatures, since the largest part of the earth's surface is covered by ocean. Very strange things come up from the ocean's depths, and we are willing, given a little help from the author, to accept that yet another creature may have surfaced in *Phantoms*. Dean Koontz is a careful writer, a painstaking researcher, and a craftsman who can always be counted on to give his readers an infrastructure of at least minimal plausibility so that they can become friendly readers, meet him half-way, and enjoy his tales, as they very clearly do. Karen Springen, writing in *Newsweek*, estimates that more than 60 million copies of Dean Koontz's books have been sold—that's a lot of friendly readers.

Strangers
(1986)

A topic that Dean Koontz returns to many times is that of parapsychology. Many of his plots involve clairvoyance, or the ability to mentally see what is happening elsewhere; telekinesis, or the ability to move objects; telepathy, or the ability to read another's mind; and such related areas as hypnotism and mind control, particularly in the form of brainwashing. A good early example of his work in this area is the novel *The Vision*, published in 1977. The protagonist of this story is Mary Bergen, a clairvoyant who assists the police on murder cases through visions in which she actually sees murderers stalking their victims. She can then direct the police to the specific locations where the stalking is taking place. At the conclusion of the story Mary discovers that she has been brainwashed as a child by her older brother. He is now seeking to kill her, and she saves herself through telepathy and telekinesis, communicating with a group of bats and directing them to kill the brother, who at this point is holding a knife on Mary.

The novel *Strangers*, published in 1986, some nine years after *The Vision*, continues to deal with these same issues, although in a far more complex way. *Strangers* is a much larger novel (681 pages) in which Koontz is able to portray a greater development of characters and give a more thorough exploration of parapsychology, its possible causes, and its ultimate effects. Reading these two novels in chronological order provides readers with insight into Koontz's development as a writer, showing how he has developed and expanded on various themes in his works.

GENRE

Like nearly all of Dean Koontz's later novels, *Strangers* is a cross-genre book that borrows conventions from several genres. As such, it fits best in the suspense category, a broad group covering works that include elements of many different genres; this category has as a defining characteristic the fact that "the characters and the reader are in a constant state of uneasy anticipation of the worst, which all too often happens" (Rosenberg and Herald 1991, 47). *Strangers* has within it elements of the mystery, in the characters' seeking, finding, and following clues to determine what has happened to them (this is particulary true of the hypnotist Pablo Jackson and his attempts to discover what lies behind the mental block implanted in the character Ginger Weiss). It has elements of the parapsychological novel, in its use of brainwashing and telekinesis. It certainly has elements of science fiction, in that the central plot device of the novel is the landing of a space ship in the Nevada desert. It is also a splendid technothriller, with much detailed discussion given to the use of highly sophisticated monitoring devices, weapons, and the like, all of it sounding authoritative and convincing. And it is a romance, with all the major characters finding true love at the end of the tale.

PLOT DEVELOPMENT

Plots can usually be divided into four parts, the original situation, the complications, the crisis or climax, and the denouement. (For a definition of each part, see Chapter 3.) In *Strangers*, the original situation is that rather odd things happen to a number of the characters. Dominick Corvaisis, an author who lives in Laguna Beach, California, has recently started sleepwalking. When he wakes up, he finds himself hiding in an out-of-the-way corner of his home, and discovers that while he was asleep he typed into his computer, over and over again, the message, "I'm scared. I'm scared." He has no idea what it is that he's afraid of, nor why he is hiding, but he tells his friend Parker Faine, "when I wake up . . . when I'm still half-asleep, I have the feeling that something's stalking me, searching for me, something that'll kill me if it finds my hidey-hole.... Yesterday, I woke up shouting, 'Stay away, stay away, stay away!' '' (51).

Like Dominick, Ginger Weiss, a cardiology resident who lives in Boston, is also afraid; she is thrown into a state of terror by the sight of a pair of black gloves, and she briefly blacks out. This is more than a scary event: what would happen if she were operating and lost consciousness? Obviously, she cannot take this lightly. Subsequently, other objects trigger blackouts too, and just as she is going into them, she hears the message, "Run or die.... Run or die" (42).

In Nevada, the character Ernie Block, who with his wife runs the Tranquility Motel in Elko, is suddenly afraid of the dark, a very recent phobia. He is fifty-two, an ex-marine and an ex-football player, and not accustomed to being frightened. Now he feels an overwhelming urge to escape: "Got to get out, get away, there won't be another chance, not another chance like this, now, go now, go, go...." (131). It is even more terrifying for him that he has no idea of what it is he needs to get away from.

While these events are happening to characters in California, Massachusetts, and Nevada, in Chicago, Father Brendan Cronin, a thirty-year-old Catholic priest, has abruptly lost his faith in God. He is overcome by rage while saying mass and throws the chalice away from himself, sweeps the communion wafers to the floor, and tears off the stole he wears to perform the mass. Just as abruptly, the anger leaves him and he too has no idea what it is that has caused him to act in this way.

Finally, in New York City, the professional thief Jack Twist, a superb operations planner who has stolen millions in his time, has just successfully completed a daring, high-risk job. He finds that he gets no pleasure from the job, and this is not at all usual for him. "When a job had been successfully concluded, Jack was usually in a grand mood for days after," but now, "something was happening to him, an inner shifting, a sea change. He felt empty, adrift, without purpose. He dared not lose his love for larceny. It was the only reason he had for living" (110–11). Like Dominick, Jack is having problems when he goes to sleep, and lately "he had been plagued by a recurring nightmare more intense than any dream he had ever known.... In the dream, he was fleeing from a man in a motorcycle helmet with a darkly tinted visor ... through unknown rooms and along amorphous corridors and, most vividly, along a deserted highway that cut through an empty moon-washed landscape" (111–12). Like the other characters, when he awakens and becomes conscious of his surroundings, he is in a state of panic.

The initial complication in *Strangers* takes place for each of the characters when they seek a rational explanation for what is happening to them. Dominick goes to his doctor to find out why he is walking in his sleep, and he is told that more than likely, it's just a reaction to stress. He changes the pattern of his days accordingly, and also uses Valium and sleeping pills to actually get some rest at night. Ginger's rational explanation is that something that she has suppressed in her past is surfacing and is causing her blackouts or fugue states; she starts a session of psychotherapy to discover what that past event is, so that she might master it. Ernie's rational explanation is that he is suffering from a phobia, an unexplained phobia that has arisen suddenly, as phobias are known to do, and he sees an expert on phobias to learn how to overcome his fear of the dark. Brendan Cronin, who believes that he has lost his faith, has undertaken a series of assignments from his pastor that are designed to help him regain it. And Jack Twist interprets his dreams as a warning in which the man in the motorcycle helmet is a policeman, out to capture Jack.

Complications intensify when none of the rational explanations works. Dominick does not stop having his dreams, and seems in danger of becoming addicted to drugs. Ginger has four psychotic episodes in five weeks, despite the fact that she is in therapy. Ernie does very well in treatment in Milwaukee, but regresses when he returns to Elko and the Tranquility Motel. And Jack, despite staging far more daring crimes in one time span than he ever has, cannot regain the thrill that this once gave him, and "wondered if he had run out of the simple courage to go on living" (112).

In their search to make sense of what is happening to them, the characters find an even more complex situation. Dominick, with the help of his friend, the painter Parker Faine, decides that the origin of his problem must lie somewhere in a trip he took a year and a half ago, after which he dramatically changed his lifestyle, going from being a timid college English professor whose main concern was with job security to being a risk taker who threw over his job in order to write and who is now on the verge of becoming a best-selling author. He doesn't understand why he made this change, and he thinks it may be related to what is happening to him now, with the sleepwalking and dreams. It seems unlikely to him that two such aberrant events would not be connected, and he decides to retrace his steps to see if he can at the same time retrace what caused these events.

The journey takes Dominick to the Tranquility Motel, where he meets with Ernie and discovers that they share some of the same images in their nightmares, and therefore they must share some of the same experiences, even though they cannot remember what those experiences were. In Boston, Ginger has lost patience—she desperately wants to get to the root cause of her fugue states so that she can go back to her work as a surgeon, and she seeks the help of Pablo Jackson, a world-famous stage magician and hypnotist who, now that he is retired, helps the police by hypnotizing witnesses so that they can recover details they have seen but no longer consciously remember. She convinces Jackson, against his will, to hypnotize her and so help her to discover why she reacts so strongly to the phenomena that trigger her psychotic episodes. What he finds is that he cannot reach these memories, that to avoid answering his questions, Ginger "seemed to be withdrawing into a sleep far deeper than her hypnotic trance, perhaps into a coma, into an oblivion where she could not hear his demanding voice. He had never encountered a reaction like this before, had never even read of such a thing. Was it possible for Ginger to *will* herself dead merely to escape his questions?" (157).

Jackson brings Ginger out of her trance and begins research on memory blocks, refusing to help her further until he understands what is going on. This leads him to an ex-director of the CIA, who explains that Jackson has met with an Azrael Block, a mental block that will instruct a subject to go into a coma and die before revealing specific information. The name of the block, Azrael, is the name of one of the angels of death. Jackson's informant tells him that he should not meddle with this situation, that an Azrael Block can be imposed only by an outside source, and this would have been done only if the matter that must remain hidden were of great significance. Further, he says that the fact that Ginger is experiencing fugue states means that whatever it was that she is suppressing is so powerful that even the Azrael Block cannot fully repress it. He warns Jackson that should he recover Ginger's memories, he himself will probably be in great danger.

Jackson determines to go ahead with Ginger's hypnosis anyway, but before he can continue, he is killed by an agent who has entered his house, thinking that he will not be there, to make duplicates of the tapes of Jackson's sessions to date with Ginger. Jackson surprises the agent, who shoots him. Ginger then enters the apartment and the agent attempts to kill her, too, but fails, because Ginger is so resourceful that she escapes him. In the meantime, Ginger has seen Dominick's picture on the back of his novel, and has recognized it. She knows that somewhere she has met him and that he is somehow involved in what is happening to her. She sends a letter to him care of his publisher, and when Dominick receives it he calls her and tells her to meet with him at the Tranquility Motel.

While all of this is going on with Ginger and Dominick, Brendan Cronin in Chicago develops the ability to cure by the laying on of his hands. He brings a young girl back to health and a policeman back from the brink of death, and it seems that he has also passed on the gift: the policeman in turn brings someone else back from the verge of death. In tracing what has happened to him in the recent past, Cronin decides that the only unusual thing he had done was make a leisurely cross-country trip the summer before last, staying for three days in a motel in Elko, Nevada. He will go back to that motel to see if he can learn something about his stay there and the changes that have taken place in him.

At the same time, an extraordinary change has also occurred in Jack Twist, who now feels compelled to give away money by the thousands to the needy of New York (first keeping enough for himself to live on in the $4 million he has salted away in Swiss bank accounts). He goes to one of his safe deposit boxes to collect the money he wants to donate, and finds in it a postcard with a picture on it of the Tranquility Motel in Elko, Nevada. Who could have put it there? How did they know he had been at the motel? Who knew his various aliases? He goes to more of his safe deposit boxes and in each finds a similar postcard. He leaves at once for Elko to find out what this means.

The stage is now set for the key characters, Dominick, Ginger, Ernie and his wife Faye, Sandy and Ned Sarver, who own the restaurant attached to the motel, Brendan Cronin, and Jack Twist to come together at the Tranquility Motel. Between them, they recreate the events of that summer a year and a half ago. They are joined by Jorja Monatella, who was also at the motel that summer and whose seven-year-old daughter is having severe nightmares—Dominick had called Jorja when he was trying to reach the people listed in the motel register for that time period.

Together, the group works out that what they saw was the landing of a spaceship, and that Ginger, Dom, and Brendan Cronin entered the ship. Dom and Brendan laid their hands on the containers of two of the creatures in the ship and in the creatures' last living moments, they passed on to the humans their healing and telekinetic powers. Acting on the basis of a government commission report warning that society cannot tolerate the knowledge that aliens have landed on earth, even if the aliens did all die in the process, the army has moved the ship into a huge underground facility in Nevada, and has brainwashed all of the witnesses (the alternative was to kill the witnesses, which at least one of the army higher-ups, Colonel Leland Falkirk, wanted to do). The group of witnesses decides to split up, with Dom, Ginger, and Jack Twist going into the underground facility and the rest going to Chicago and Boston, where they will contact the media and tell the world what has happened in Nevada.

Dom, Ginger, and Jack succeed in breaking into the facility, but the others are arrested by special army troops before they can carry out their part of the plan. They are joined by Dom's friend Parker Faine who, along with Brendan Cronin's pastor, has come to join the witnesses. Both have been shot by the troops, with Faine surviving because Brendan healed him but the pastor dying before Brendan can reach him. All are taken to the underground facility. While these events are happening, the reader learns that the lead scientist on the project and the general in charge of the place were responsible for placing the postcards in Jack Twist's safe deposit boxes. They have come to believe that the spaceship and its arrival are wonderful news for the people of earth, and that everyone must know of this miracle.

All of the questions have now been answered—what happened to the characters and why it happened—and the stage is set for the climax. Here, Colonel Falkirk confronts the witnesses, the lead scientist, and the general, telling them that he knows they are no longer human, that they have been taken over by the aliens. He has set two small nuclear devices to destroy the ship and everyone who has had any contact with it, including everyone in the facility as well as the facility itself. Once the bombs are set, they cannot be disarmed. They will go off in fifteen minutes. Brendan and Dom decide that their only hope is to use their telekinetic powers to disarm the devices. Dom disarms one, but Brendan cannot disarm the other—he can't focus on it. However, at the last minute Parker Faine, who was cured by Brendan and as a result now has the same power as Brendan has, disarms the second device and everyone is saved, with the exception of Colonel Falkirk, who commits suicide rather than be, as he imagines, changed into an alien.

In the denouement, the characters discuss the significance of the knowledge that has been brought to them by the spaceship. Human beings have been brought the power of healing so that we can live virtually forever, and we have been given this gift by a benevolent race that has dedicated its people to sending out ships like this one to any intelligent beings it locates in the cosmos; doing so is fundamental to the society's structure and beliefs, to what we would think of as its religion. Soon the witnesses will tell the world of this wonder, and soon the world will be changed. In the meantime, everyone is cured. Dom no longer has nightmares and has fallen in love with Ginger; Ginger no longer suffers from fugues and has fallen in love with Dom. Brendan Cronin has recovered his faith, and Jack Twist now has a purpose in living, since he has fallen in love with Jorja, who has also fallen in love with him. Her daughter Marcie no longer has nightmares, and has gained a father in Jack. Sandy and Ned decide to have a child, and Ernie will never again fear the dark.

CHARACTER DEVELOPMENT

In *Strangers*, nearly every character changes in some way and is therefore dynamic. Because a large group of witnesses take part in the unravelling of the story, the novel has many protagonists rather than the usual one or two. If we count only the leading characters, there are still Dom, Ginger, Jack, Brendan, and Ernie in major roles and Faye, Sandy, Ned, Jorja, Brendan's pastor Father Wycazik, Dom's friend Parker, and the hypnotist Pablo Jackson in minor but significant roles. This makes twelve protagonists.

The two most important characters are Dominick Corvaisis and Ginger Weiss. Dominick, who opens the novel, is basically a flat character, since his background is sketched in rather than examined in depth. He was brought up in foster homes, but no other information is offered. As an adult Dom was initially a timid, conservative person whose main objective was security. An English teacher at the University of Portland in Oregon, he wrote stories that he never sent out for publication. His main concern was that he be granted tenure, which would have virtually guaranteed him job security for the rest of his life, but Dom was so afraid that he would be denied tenure he left his job and went to a much smaller, more isolated school in Utah, where he was promised tenure. Once there, Dom quit the new job before it ever began and concentrated on writing a novel that to his astonishment was bought at once, for a very good price, by a top publisher. The book is now on the verge of becoming a best-seller, and Dom is about to become famous.

Until the very end of the novel, Dom has no idea why he threw over his job and acted in such a highly uncharacteristic way. It is only in the denouement that he and the reader learn that this was his reaction to having witnessed the landing of the space ship. The scope of its achievement in traveling millions of miles over thousands upon thousands of years is so extraordinary that it suddenly makes things like job security and tenure seem unimaginably insignificant, and this insight frees Dom to pursue his writing, even though the insight is hidden from him for almost two years by the brainwashing he underwent. Thus, although for most of the book he does not know why he has changed, he is a dynamic character because when he recognizes the catalyst of the change, he also recognizes its validity. The insight he has gained into himself causes him to see both himself and the world differently, and gaining such self-knowledge is a good rule-of-thumb definition for a dynamic character.

The second major protagonist is Ginger Weiss. She is the best example of a well-rounded character in *Strangers*, since there is a good deal of information on her childhood, her parents, the people who were significant in her life, her choice of career, and the like. She is one of those people who has been blessed with a loving home, superior intelligence, and exceptional good looks; while she is not wealthy, she has never lived in poverty. She is just about to complete her residency in surgery when she begins to have psychotic attacks. Clearly, if these continue she will never be able to be a surgeon—she would never dare operate if at any moment she might have an attack. The attacks are highly uncharacteristic of the self-confident, highly competent Ginger, who has never failed at anything, let alone believed that she could fail. She is a courageous woman and accepts the threat of possible death in working to recover the memories that lie behind her attacks. When at last she does recover them, they too bring about a change in her, since she now sees the possibility of a world where her profession and her skills will be redundant, a world in which people can be healed by touch and where everyone can have this touch. Ginger welcomes this vision and will work to make it a reality because it is more important—it is healing of a different order—than anything she has ever previously envisioned. Thus, she is a dynamic character because her insights lead her to reexamine and reevaluate one of the central elements of her life, her profession.

Jack Twist, the professional thief, is also a major protagonist, since it is his knowledge and planning ability that enables the witnesses to escape from the motel and take on the military establishment. Like Dom, Twist is a relatively flat character. We know nothing about his childhood, his friends, or why he chose the military as a profession—the fact that he was a soldier is simply a convenient way of explaining how he has attained his extraordinary skills and knowledge of weapons. By the same token, his supposed reason for resorting to theft is that it enables him to pay the horrendous medical fees for his beloved wife, who has been in a coma for eight years, and it also allows him to strike back at a society that, as he sees it, exploited him as a soldier and a citizen. Again, these are convenient devices for allowing the reader to accept Twist's dishonesty without having to think of him as a dishonest person: he's doing good things with the money he steals and, besides, bad things were done to him. The suggestion is that in a good world, he would be a good man.

The real focus of Jack Twist's activities is on how exciting they are, rather than on how dishonest they are. His first job in the novel is robbing a Mafia collection point of millions of dollars in laundered drug money, and the reader can hardly feel that some terrible harm has been done. The scene itself is one of the best in the book—the Mafia walk in on the robbery, and how Jack and his men escape is the stuff of pure adventure. Everyone's adrenaline surges here, including the reader's. The underlying suggestion is that Jack Twist is a professional thief because it is so exciting to be one, and that the rationale for his theft is just window-dressing that allows us to enjoy the excitement and adventure. Of all the major characters, Jack undergoes the most radical change: he stops enjoying planning and undertaking jobs, although he has no idea why this is so. Again, it is ultimately as a result of his witnessing of the spaceship. Given the awesomeness of its achievement, knocking over a Mafia warehouse is very small stuff, and at the end of the novel it is clear that Jack is done with his days of crime, although he certainly intends to benefit by living in comfort for the rest of his life.

The other major protagonist is the priest, Brendan Cronin. Essentially a flat character, Cronin exists for the reader only as a priest. We know of his training, background, and experience in the priesthood, and very little else about him. However, because he exists only in terms of his profession, it is doubly puzzling when he loses his faith—this is the very center of his being, both for himself and for the reader's perception of him. This is, of course, a dramatic change, making him a dynamic character. But as with the other protagonists, he understands the cause of this change only at the end of the novel, when he sees the spaceship and realizes that it has brought him an understanding of God. To have seen such evidence of God's work and then to have it suppressed by brainwashing is what has caused his loss of faith, and regaining the knowledge of what he experienced gives him back the knowledge of God, the basis of his faith.

The remaining protagonists play less significant roles, but are also changed by their witnessing of the spaceship. Ernie Block, who with his wife Faye owns the Tranquility Motel, is a good example of a stock character. He is a stereotype of the ex-marine—big, strong, silent, and brave, a loyal husband and friend. Despite his being a stock character, he is dynamic: he has, of all things, become terrified of the dark. Anyone less likely to experience such a fear is hard to imagine, and at the end of the novel he learns that, indeed, he has no fear of the dark. His fear is based on what happened to him in the dark, when he became the subject of brainwashing. This insight frees him from his phobias, but he does not go back to being the same person he was before. Like the other witnesses, he has experienced the wonder of the spaceship and understands that there are other possibilities for mankind as a result of that alien contact.

His wife, Faye, is another stock character—the strong, supportive wife. She is one of the book's few static characters, since she has no memory of the spacecraft and has undergone no change as a result of it. In this she is like Ned Sarver, husband to Sandy, with whom he runs the Tranquility Grill. Ned is the strong, supportive husband, has no memory of the events, and has undergone no change. His wife, Sandy, is more developed: her background as a sexually abused child is sensitively drawn. While it is all we know about her, it is so painful to think of a child hurt in this way that it has the effect of making her a round character—we fill in the empty spaces in our concern that victimizing children in this way could and does happen. Sandy is also dynamic, and for her the change is positive long before she has any idea of why it has occurred. She becomes confident, loving, and able to enjoy sex for the first time in her life. In the denouement she discovers that this came of her seeing the spaceship and realizing how insignificant a single human being is—how weak and puny her father, who caused her so much pain, really is and how little ability he has to hurt her now. She is freed when her giant ogre of a father becomes infintesimal in the overall scheme of things. At the end of the novel Sandy decides to have a child, and while this might have been an overly sentimental moment, it is not. The reader experiences it as an affirmation of life and of survival, of caring and loving on the part of someone who as a child was neither cared for nor loved.

Like Faye Block, Jorja Monatella would seem to be a static character, since she has no recollection of ever having seen the spaceship and so can gain no insight from the experience. But she is in fact a dynamic character, having gained insight into her own life and the possibilities open to her from the example of Ginger Weiss. Jorja met Ginger in Nevada, just before the experiences at the Tranquility Motel, when Ginger stopped on the highway to help Jorja's daughter, Marcie (the child had fallen down an embankment). Jorja, up to now a cocktail waitress who believes that such jobs are the only ones open to her, watches Ginger and realizes that like Ginger, she can do other things with her life. If someone as pretty, small, and delicate as Ginger can also be self-confident, in control, and taking charge, then maybe Jorja can be this way, too—maybe she is not doomed to be a bimbo and serve drinks for the rest of her life. Basically a minor character, Jorja is a good example of how small roles can be fleshed out to create rounded characters. In the short space given to her Koontz does a fine job of sketching in her job and her attitude toward it, her horrendous parents and her feelings toward them, her ex-husband and his attraction for her (given parents like hers, anyone would look attractive), and her feelings toward her child. At the end of the novel, when Jorja is paired up with Jack Twist, the reader hopes that this will not put an end to Jorja's newfound dreams for herself, that she will continue to pursue a life of her own.

There are three other significant positive characters, although none of them was a witness to the spaceship. These are Father Wycazik, Brendan Cronin's rector, a flat, static character who represents faith that cannot be shaken. Dom Corvaisis's friend, Parker Faine, is another flat, static character, who represents the values of loyalty and friendship. He is one of the few examples in Koontz's work of a friend (most of Koontz's characters are loners who, when they bond, do so with someone of the opposite sex in a romantic liaison). And finally Pablo Jackson, the hypnotist who helps Ginger to uncover her memories, is also a flat, static character, but the little we are given of his background is provocative and makes us want to learn more about him. He is the child of African Americans who lived as expatriots in France, and he is also the god-child of Pablo Picasso, for whom he is named. Now in his eighties, he has had a long, successful career as a stage magician in Europe. His bravery and kindness, along with his exotic background, give him more weight as a character than the few scenes in which he actually appears seem to warrant. At his death we miss him—we'd like to see more of him in the story.

Although *Strangers* has many protagonists, it has only one villian, Colonel Leland Falkirk, and he is not introduced until more than halfway through the book, since it isn't until then that the other characters can recall enough of the events that have taken place to be able to pinpoint him. At first glance he seems to be a stock character, the military figure in a position of such great authority that there are no checks on him or her, a figure who has quietly gone mad and who can now bring total destruction upon the rest of humanity (or at least, upon those in the character's orbit). This figure appears in much popular culture, from the novels *Mutiny on the Bounty* and *The Caine Mutiny* to the films *Dr. Strangelove* and *Apocalypse Now.* However, there is more to Falkirk than a simple outline. Koontz takes care to fill in his background so that the reader understands why it is that Falkirk might see pain in a positive light, and why he would see himself as being very brave and acting in the best interests of mankind by destroying the spaceship and everyone who has had contact with it. Nonetheless, Falkirk is a flat character. All that is known about him is that his parents were religious fanatics who beat him in the name of God, and that he has reacted by becoming a bit claustrophobic and more than a bit paranoid, anti-religious, and obsessed with being in control. Surely there would have been other influences on his life, but this is all we have. Even so, Falkirk is a dynamic character. As a result of his contact with the spaceship, he has come to see that he enjoys the pain he inflicts on himself, that it is done not simply to temper him and make him stronger but also because he receives pleasure from it. This is a new insight for Falkirk, one not available to him at the beginning of the novel.

SETTING

The setting of a Dean Koontz novel serves primarily as a backdrop for the action of the characters rather than as a motivating force in and of itself. In *Strangers*, most of the settings are cities throughout the United States: Laguna Beach, Boston, Chicago, and New York City. These could just as easily be any other cities that were geographically separated, since the point is how widespread they are and how unlikely it is that in the normal course of events, someone in Chicago would have a dream with elements in that are exactly like those of someone in California. The settings are intended to raise the question of what it is that has happened to affect people on a national scale—a question that is answered in yet another unnatural setting, the man-made cavern holding the spaceship in Nevada.

One location that could not be easily exchanged with any other is the natural setting composed of the barrens of Nevada, a desolate, empty, desertlike area. This is an ideal place for a spaceship to land and be subsequently hidden. If instead the spaceship had landed at Chicago's O'Hare airport, the busiest airport in the world, there is little chance that it could have been kept secret from the rest of the country. Thus, the Nevada setting adds credibility to the story. The fact that the exact landing spot exerts a powerful pull on some of the witnesses adds to the sense of how dramatic and overwhelming the event was, since the pull exists even though these characters no longer have conscious memories of what happened here. The Tranquility Motel also works to give credibility to the story. It is so far from any town or settlement that whatever happened there could indeed be contained and hidden from outsiders. And, of course, a motel is a perfect place to have a group of strangers come together and then go their separate ways.

One other artificial setting that is most effective is the uniform that Jorja Monatella is required to wear in her job as a cocktail waitress: "a little red nothing, cut high in the crotch and hips, very low at the bustline, smaller than a bathing suit. An elastic corset was built in to minimize the waistline and emphasize the breasts. . . . The getup made you look almost freakishly erotic" (168). If that doesn't raise a woman's consciousness about being a sex object, nothing will, and it is this consciousness that prepares the way for Jorja to model herself after Ginger Weiss.

POINT OF VIEW

Dean Koontz's point of view of choice seems to be third-person omniscient, in which an unknown narrator who can see into the minds of all the characters tells the story and includes the thoughts of many people. In *Strangers*, this point of view allows the reader to see the changes that have taken place in each of the characters and how they react to those changes. It allows us to see the background of a character such as Leland Falkirk, a background that he would be most reluctant to disclose. It allows us to see the great pleasure Jack Twist takes in planning and carrying out his heists, something he would probably not reveal for fear of making himself vulnerable. We understand the terrible fear of Ernie Block, who can barely admit to himself that he is afraid of the dark. We can overhear the conversations of Dr. Miles Bennell and General Alvarado in the underground cavern and so be convinced that Falkirk really has gone mad, that there is nothing to fear from the spaceship. A first-person point of view would simply not work here, since it would be limited to only one character and too much that is significant would be hidden from that character. Third-person limited might work, since it can be divided among a number of characters, with each telling the story from his or her point of view. But there are a great many characters in *Strangers*, all of whom have been affected by the alien landing, and it would be cumbersome to shift from one mind to another to understand what is happening overall, especially since the individual characters are all suffering from memory blocks. For the same reason, third-person dramatic would not work since it is essential that the reader be aware of the mental reactions of the characters, especially their reactions to their dreams and their attempts to recover their memories. We would be at a complete loss if we had to figure out what those reactions were from what people were doing and saying, since they are not acting rationally and they themselves do not understand their reactions. Given these considerations, third-person omniscient is both the most practical and the most effective choice for telling this multilayered story.

THEMATIC ISSUES

The theme seems to be clearly stated in the denouement, when the characters are discussing the significance of what has occurred and Ginger thinks that now a great bond will be formed among all human beings—that we will no longer be strangers to one another because among us we will have defeated death. By learning the techniques of healing, we will live with one another for incredibly long time spans, and this in and of itself will create the bond. If our essential loneliness is based on the fact that we are born and die alone, then one half of the equation will have been removed and, therefore, we will learn to share life rather than to fear death. It is curious that Koontz has so clearly spelled out the theme rather than, as he usually does, leaving it for readers to arrive at for themselves. Perhaps the point of being so specific is precisely to alert the reader to be careful of the obvious—to question whether this really is the theme of the novel, and if it is not, to challenge readers to arrive at a second theme that has not been as carefully laid out for them.

Assuming that the theme is not specifically identified for readers—that instead Koontz is challenging us to work it out for ourselves—one possible candidate for the theme might derive from the title of the novel: the word *strangers*. Surely all human beings from earliest times have feared strangers; like death, they are the ultimate unknown. Many cultures have in their languages two different words for people—one for themselves and another that identifies those who are not of their group, tribe, or culture. Many wars have been fought on the basis that one group of people is so different from another as to constitute a threat to its very existence. Yet scientific analysis of the human race shows that we have far more in common with one another, regardless of our racial or ethnic backgrounds, than we have differences. When the spaceship lands in Nevada, Colonel Falkirk sees it as a mortal threat—as something that will destroy our humanity—because it is different. If we were indeed to fear that which is different, an alien spaceship thousands and thousands of years old, filled with dead and dying creatures like nothing ever seen on earth, would seem to be about as different as anything on earth can get. Falkirk's view is rejected, though, and the spaceship is seen instead as a great boon to mankind. The extraterrestrial strangers bring us the gift of bonding together. Perhaps Koontz's underlying theme, then, is that we have nothing to fear from that which seems strange, different, or alien; perhaps embracing the unknown is what will allow us to embrace one another.

ALTERNATIVE READING: A FEMINIST ANALYSIS

Feminism as a type of literary analysis takes it energy from the women's movement of the 1960s, a movement that paralleled the movement for civil rights among such marginalized groups as Native Americans, African Americans, and Hispanic Americans. As a social movement, feminism dates back to the late eighteenth century and particularly to Mary Wollstonecraft's *A Vindication of the Rights of Women* (1792). Feminism develops its aesthetic aspect much later than this, with the publication of the novelist Virginia Woolf's *A Room of One's Own* (1929), in which Woolf explored the concept of women as writers and the obstacles they faced. These two strands of feminism, the political and the aesthetic, have in common that each examines the limits placed on women by the society around them, a society that assumes such limits are not arbitrarily imposed but are natural, imposed by nature and biology.

One of the most significant voices in exposing the fallacy of natural biological limitations was that of the French philosopher Simone de Beauvoir, whose *The Second Sex* (1949) explored the status of women in society. De Beauvoir critiqued not only this status, but showed how it served to create a self-image for women that helped keep them subservient. We are all products of our culture, and we tend to accept its standards and evaluations as our own. If these tell us that we are inferior, we tend to think of ourselves as inferior. Breaking out of this pattern is very difficult, and it is a testament to the work of de Beauvoir that, living within the pattern, she was able to see it as socially constructed rather than as biologically mandated. One aspect of de Beauvoir's work was the examination of women in the literature of male writers—an examination that turned on the concept of gender, in which men were describing the appropriate roles for women. These were roles that, as feminists ever since have shown, unnecessarily limit opportunities for women in the name of what is natural and innate.

From these two main strands of feminism—the political strand, which examines the place of women as fellow citizens and focuses on their legal rights, and the aesthetic strand, which examines the portrayal of women in art and literature—comes the work of such contemporary feminist critics as Elaine Showalter, who has created the concept of "gynocriticism," which examines not only the actual writings of women but also the social and economic conditions under which these works were produced. In this way, feminist criticism is an inclusive criticism, embracing economic approaches, cultural approaches, and biographical and historical approaches, as well as traditional studies of the work of literature in and of itself. In all of these areas it has made a strong contribution to our understanding of gender issues, both male and female. Today, one school of feminism, represented by such French theorists as Julia Kristeva and Helene Cixous, concerns itself primarily with issues of gender, postulating that gender is indeed biological and determines how women see the world, how they interpret it in language, as both writers and readers. A central task of this group is to explore the concept of an innate language of women—one biologically determined by gender.

A second school of feminist criticism, identified with British and American feminists, concerns itself primarily with studies by and about women, and makes the assumption that such studies are open to all objective readers and critics, regardless of gender. For this school, gender does not determine a critic's ability to explore the world of literature from the perspective of how women are presented in that world (or sometimes, excluded from it) as creators as well as participants. The underlying assumption of this school is that any honest, objective reader or critic can perform a feminist analysis of a text.

A final result of the feminist movement has been the rediscovery of women's writing, from journals, letters, and diaries (the genres that were traditionally most accessible to women) to novels that were published but then forgotten for decades. Many of these have now been republished, and their availability has broadened the field of literature, bringing the world of women into the mainstream world of all human experience.

In looking at the part that gender plays in the novels of Dean Koontz, it is notable that all of the works covered here have strong women characters who carry much of the weight of the narrative (see, for example, *Dark Rivers of the Heart*, Chapter 10). Of these, *Strangers* lends itself particularly well to a feminist analysis because it has many different women from varied backgrounds in key roles. In every case, these women are viewed as equals to corresponding male characters, although there are times when they need to remind the men that they are indeed equals. The major woman character is Ginger Weiss. She is a doctor, a profession that was until recently closed to women; within that profession she is in a specialty that is primarily a male one, since she is a heart surgeon rather than, say, a pediatrician or an obstetrician—specialties that relate much more closely to the traditional female roles of mother and wife. She is an only child and an orphan, which means that she is fully responsible for herself. Ginger is physically small and exceptionally pretty, and she understands full well that this can be a barrier for a woman. Because she is a woman, people often misjudge her, assuming her to be far less capable and intelligent than she is. In other words, they look at her and judge her as an object, something decorative rather than as a unique person with her own unique characteristics. However, when the hypnotist Pablo Jackson meets Ginger, he decides that her face is a balance of feminine beauty and masculine strength, which is somewhat difficult to imagine although it is clearly intended as a compliment.

No one in the novel seems surprised at Ginger's profession. When she begins to suffer from psychotic states, no one suggests that she is finding the stress of her work to be too much, which would have been a typical reaction of both males and females just a few decades ago, when women were seen as the "weaker" sex—mentally, emotionally, and physically. Ginger has great physical bravery, as she proves by overpowering a mugger and, later, by escaping from Jackson's killer. She knows how to use handguns and she also knows her own worth. When, at the end of the story, Jack Twist is working out a plan for Dom, Ned, and him to enter the underground military facility, Ginger tells Jack that he really isn't thinking straight in considering only men for the expedition—that in fact they need her on the team since she is a doctor and the mission is a dangerous one. She also points out that if they are to have a public relations impact as hostages, this will be stronger if a young woman is among the hostages. Thus, she not only knows her value as an individual, but also understands how stereotypes about woman can help the group. Finally, Ginger is recognized as a role model by Jorja, the cocktail waitress who sees both Ginger and Jack as born leaders. This comparison is an interesting one, since Jack is the strongest male character in the novel in terms of such cultural stereotypes as fighting, survival, and strategizing skills, and for Ginger to be like him makes her an equally strong character.

Other women in the novel have lesser roles than Ginger, but within these roles they are treated as equals by the other characters in the story. Rita Hannaby, the upper-middle-class wife of an eminent heart surgeon, is respected for having done charity work that has made a difference. Faye, Ernie Block's wife, might be seen as the stereotypical devoted wife except that Ernie is just as devoted to her as she is to him: each relies equally on the other. Jorja Monatella, who has always thought of herself as a menial, takes strength from sisterhood, seeing in Ginger the image of a different kind of woman—a kind of woman that Jorja can aspire to being. After all, if one woman can make something of herself, then another can, and Jorja enrolls in college classes to begin her recreation of herself. Finally, Sandy Sarver, who has been victimized and sexually abused by her father, is able to put these terrible experiences behind her because of the insights she has after seeing the spaceship. This is in direct contrast to the case of Colonel Falkirk, also physically abused as a child by his fanatical parents, who retreats further and further into paranoia, even though he has also seen the spaceship.

Overall, in looking at these women characters, we find that they are consistent with their class and background and, at the same time, respected by those around them for their values and actions. Koontz has said of his depiction of women, "I've been criticized by a few—all male—writers for always having a major role for a woman in each of my books. . . . In *reality* women are half the world, involved in every aspect of life; if you can't portray them that way in fiction, then you can't be writing seriously" (Gorman interview, 41).

Watchers
(1987)

Of the many suspense novels that Dean Koontz has written, *Watchers* is without doubt one of the most beloved by readers. Nearly every fan of Koontz lists it as a favorite, and Koontz himself says of it, "It was a difficult book to write but I was never for a moment in despair or consumed by doubt. I knew the story and the characters worked, scene by scene, and that I had my hands on special material. From first page to last, writing that book was a transcendent, joyous, indescribable experience. Floods of blood and sweat, you understand, but unremitting joy, as well. . . . The story came like a great wide river, flowing smooth and swift, and for the whole ride I knew I was going somewhere special" (Gorman interview, 46–47). The novel is exceptionally well structured, with all the component parts coming together in a unified whole. This is no small achievement in a work of almost 500 pages.

GENRE

Like nearly all of Dean Koontz's later novels, *Watchers* is a cross-genre book that uses conventions from several genres. It fits best in the suspense category, a broad category covering works that include elements of many different genres. This category has as a defining characteristic the fact that "the characters and the reader are in a constant state of

uneasy anticipation of the worst, which all too often happens" (Rosenberg and Herald 1991, 47). *Watchers* has within it elements of the science
fiction genre of hard science in the genetic engineering that brings about
the monster, The Outsider. It is also a love story in the developing relationship between the protagonists, a technothriller in its careful descriptions of weapons and security measures, a police procedural in the
accurate descriptions of the way in which the NSA agents work, a gang-
ster story in the person of the hitman Vince Nasco, and overriding all of
this, an inspiring dog story whose suspense is based on a series of threats
to a very special dog.

PLOT DEVELOPMENT

In *Watchers*, the original situation is that the hero or protagonist, Travis
Cornell, is in despair, living a life that feels pointless and without meaning." Everyone close to him has died. His mother died in childbirth;
when he was ten years old, his beloved older brother drowned in an
accident that he witnessed; when he was fourteen, his father was killed
in an automobile accident; as an adult he went into the Special Forces,
and the nine other members of his ten-member team were killed; and
after he returned to civilian life, his wife of ten months died of cancer.
He has come to believe that he is a jinx, that everyone he may ever love
is doomed to die. When the novel opens, Travis has gone hunting rattlesnakes in the Santa Ana foothills of California, attempting to recover
one of the pleasures of his childhood.

In *Watchers* the initial complication Travis must face is the appearance of a golden retriever who will not let him go deeper into the forest. Although it is very friendly to him, the dog turns hostile and bars
Travis's way when he tries to penetrate the woods. Eventually he realizes that the dog is warning him of unknown danger ahead (a danger that Koontz emphasizes by having the forest become unnaturally
still, with all its creatures silent, waiting, and watching). Travis leaves
the forest with the retriever, and this begins a whole series of further
complications. First Travis learns that the retriever is exceptionally intelligent, and that he has escaped from Banodyne, a DNA research facility where he was bred to have the physical characteristics and
personality of a dog combined with an almost human level of intelligence. Also escaped from the same laboratory is The Outsider, another

genetically engineered super-intelligent animal. But unlike the dog (whom Travis names Einstein in recognition of his intellectual abilities), The Outsider has been bred to be a killer. He hates the dog, and is the danger that was waiting in the Santa Ana foothills: he is intent on finding and killing Einstein.

The escape of the two super-animals brings in the National Security Agency (NSA), a government intelligence agency whose task is to recover them at once, since they are the product of a top-secret defense project. At the same time the Soviets have learned of the project and are in the process of destroying all information concerning it. They burn down the part of the lab holding records and files of the experiments, and hire a hitman to kill every scientist with direct information about the project. This hitman, Vince Nasco, a contract killer with Mafia connections, becomes curious about why he is killing scientists and interrogates his last victims, learning about the Banodyne project and in particular, about the dog, Einstein. Nasco determines to capture the dog for himself and then ransom it to the highest bidder. Thus, poor Einstein now has The Outsider, the NSA, and a contract killer searching for him and only Travis protecting him, but Travis has a good deal to offer in the role of protector: he is an ex-Special Forces soldier, with the weapons, surveillance, and survival training that go with that role. He loves Einstein, and after the long series of deaths in his life, he desperately needs to have something he loves survive and flourish.

While all of this is going on, Einstein meets Nora Devon, a thirty-year-old orphaned recluse, in a park where Travis has taken him. Einstein and Nora immediately bond. Subsequently he saves her from a rapist (he is a great dog) and Nora and Travis fall in love. The three become a family, intent on staying together and keeping Einstein from being captured and returned to the lab, and much clever, well-constructed escaping of various traps follows.

In the climax, Nora is kidnapped by the contract killer, the contract killer is killed by Travis, Einstein is killed by The Outsider, and The Outsider is killed by Travis.

Finally, in the denouement the reader learns that Einstein is still alive—that he was not killed but only badly wounded by The Outsider. One of the NSA agents knows this, but he too has fallen under Einstein's spell and files a report listing the dog as dead and the case is closed. Nora, Travis, and Einstein can now live happily ever after.

CHARACTER DEVELOPMENT

Even though it is meticulously plotted and depends heavily on linear development from one incident to the next, *Watchers* is also rich in character, with even minor figures given personality and substance. The major protagonist of the novel is Travis Cornell, a round (fully developed) character since we have so much information on his background and state of mind. Specifically, we know of his despair and its causes, and we know of the skills he has that qualify him to be Einstein's rescuer. He is also a dynamic character, since he changes over the course of the novel, beginning as someone who has denied himself all close social contact and ending as someone committed to others.

In addition to Travis, *Watchers* has two other protagonists: Nora Devon and the dog Einstein. Nora is somewhat of a flat (one-dimensional) character in that we are given a simplistic background for her to explain her reclusiveness; however, she is also a dynamic character, since she changes over the course of the novel, developing into a social person who is giving to others and capable of rich interpersonal relationships. And because she is a central agent in her own development, she goes from being a passive to an active character.

The third protagonist, the dog Einstein, can certainly be described as a well-rounded character, since we know a great deal about his background; however, he is a static character since he does not change during the course of the novel, beginning and ending as a genius dog.

One other positive character who, despite a small role, is drawn as round and dynamic is the NSA agent Lemuel Johnson. Initially he is an antagonist, out to capture Einstein and return him to the lab. Johnson's background as the success-driven son of a successful African-American businessman is well described, making the reader afraid that he will indeed succeed in capturing Einstein, since he is an exceptionally good agent who cannot tolerate failure. And he is also a dynamic character since, by the novel's end, he no longer accepts his father's standards and has resigned from the NSA, having filed a report he knows to be false to protect the dog and leave it in peace. He has moved from an antagonist to a protagonist, and never again will he be driven by the need to succeed in someone else's eyes. It is significant that each of these positive human characters is dynamic. In this way, Koontz demonstrates the special quality of Einstein, because it is association with Einstein that becomes the catalyst for each person's change. Only Einstein is static, and he is a character who has no need of change: he is wonderful as he is.

Vince Nasco, the primary human antagonist in *Watchers*, is a flat character, since almost the only information we have about him is that he thoroughly enjoys his work as a contract killer and thinks "how lucky he was to have found a way to make murder his business, to be paid for what he would have done anyway" (50). He believes that each killing he does increases his own longevity, since he is convinced that his victims' life essences pass to him at the moment of their deaths, giving him many lives to live. He's not sure if he has yet reached immortality, but he knows he must be close. At the end of the novel he ends up dead, believing even in the last moment before his death that some mistake has been made—he wasn't supposed to be mortal. Thus, he is a static character; from the beginnning to the end, no change takes place in his character or in his perception of reality.

In the same way that the protagonist Travis Cornell has a nonhuman coprotagonist in the dog Einstein, the antagonist Vince Nasco is paired with a nonhuman antagonist, The Outsider. If it is not human, it is also not quite animal, since Koontz always refers to The Outsider as "it." Nasco and The Outsider seek the same goal—the capture of the dog— although each is unaware of the other. Unlike Nasco, The Outsider is a round character, however. We know of its genesis as a genetically programmed creature at Banodyne. We know of its loathing for itself because it is aware of how extraordinarily ugly it is. We see the terrible loneliness of The Outsider. Finally, we know of its hatred for the dog, who, although he too is genetically engineered, is normal in his appearance and so is not doomed to a lonely life as an outsider. The complex character of The Outsider is developed through a very moving scene describing its lair in the forest: "Apparently, The Outsider had stolen . . . packs of candy somewhere along the way. The strange thing was that the wrappers were not crumpled but were smoothed out and laid flat on the floor along the back wall. . . . Perhaps The Outsider liked the bright colors of the wrappers. Or perhaps it kept them to remind itself of the pleasure that the candy had given it because, once those treats were gone, there was not much other pleasure to be had in the hard life to which it had been driven" (264). The Outsider has survived by eating wild amimals, but it has hidden the bones of these animals way in back in its cave and has arranged for itself a display of colorful, shining objects. NSA agent Lem Johnson, on seeing this, thinks that perhaps despite The Outsider's profound otherness, it can appreciate beauty and has "a desire to live not as an animal but as a thinking being in an ambience at least lightly touched by civilization" (265). As a troubled monster, The Outsider is part of a long line of troubled monsters beginning with Mary Shelley's *Frankenstein*, and we respond to it with great pity as well as with great fear. At the novel's end, there is some indication that The Outsider may be a dynamic character, since ultimately it does not kill Einstein but only severely wounds him. Travis speculates that in these final moments, The Outsider may have found mercy in itself and, in doing so, may have recognized the remote possibility of fellowship with other living beings: "Seeing itself as like others, perhaps it could not kill Einstein" (482).

Another indication of the care that Koontz has taken with characters in *Watchers* is his treatment of minor figures whose appearance in the novel is momentary and who therefore might reasonably have been drawn as stock figures only. Instead, even these are given defining characteristics that individualize them. A good example of such a single-purpose character is Johnny "The Wire" Santini, a Mafia member who lives in a huge Art Deco beach house in San Clemente. He takes up a total of only 7 pages in a 483-page novel, and since he shares these with two other characters, he doesn't even have the 7 pages to himself, yet Koontz has taken the trouble to tell the reader what sort of house Johnny lives in. Koontz then goes on to make use of this setting by describing what it shows of The Wire's character: "he liked Art Deco because it reminded him of the Roaring Twenties, and he liked the twenties because that was the romantic era of legendary gangsters." He sees himself as part of a great romantic tradition, "mystical kin to Jesse James, Dillinger, Al Capone, the Dalton boys, Lucky Luciano" (149).

The Wire has been in the mob all his life, and over the years has grown somewhat jaded, so with the advent of computers, Johnny has become the mob's top computer hacker. "If you wanted to run a major credit-card scam, charging a million bucks worth of purchases to other people's American Express accounts, Johnny The Wire could suck some suitable names and credit histories out of TRW's files and matching card numbers from American Express's data banks, and you were in business" (152). We learn all of this in the single visit that Vince Nasco makes to Johnny to have him search files for Travis and Nora's new identities. Running the search is Johnny's only function in the novel, and there is no plot necessity for the detailed information given about him. It is clear that Koontz has included the additional information because he is having fun with the character of Johnny The Wire, and so too does the reader. Small scenes such as these continually appear in the novel, adding subtly to its overall suspense and, in the process, giving this very long work freshness and variety.

SETTING

Dean Koontz is usually very traditional in his use of setting, placing it primarily as a backdrop for the action rather than as a motivating force. In *Watchers*, a memorable natural setting is The Outsider's lair, and the contrast of this natural den with the man-made items found within it— candy wrappers and decorative objects—shows the complexity of The Outsider, a creature who is more than animal and less than human. Natural setting is also used to herald the coming of death, as in the torrential rainstorm that precedes the novel's climax.

Throughout *Watchers*, Koontz also makes strong use of artificial setting as a device to show character. There is a fine scene in San Francisco's Tenderloin district, an area of bars and strip clubs, seen from the point of view of Nora Devon, who has never been out of suburban Santa Barbara. Nora enables us to see the sleaziness of the area through innocent eyes reacting in wonder—she has no context for comprehending a place like this, and her reaction to it emphasizes both its corruption and her own extraordinarily sheltered life. Koontz effectively marks Nora's character change from a reclusive person to someone becoming attached to Travis and Einstein by having her shed the drab dresses she wears at the beginning of the novel for colorful shorts and halters. Homes are used to represent the type of people who live in them, from Johnny The Wire's Art Deco mansion to the casual, comfortable home of a veterinarian who turns out to be a casual, comfortable man, and yet another champion of Einstein.

POINT OF VIEW

Dean Koontz's point of view of choice seems to be third-person omniscient, in which an unknown narrator who can see into the minds of all the characters tells the story and includes the thoughts of many people. In *Watchers*, this point of view allows the reader to know how Vince Nasco feels about killing, something he tells no one. It allows us to see how very reclusive Nora is, something she could not tell us because of her very reclusiveness. It makes us aware of the ambivalence that Lem Johnson feels toward his job, something he only gradually comes to realize himself. And most of all, this point of view shows us what an extraordinary dog Einstein is because through it, Koontz can show the reactions of everyone who comes into contact with him. We never see into the mind of Einstein, though, and this is as it should be: it is Einstein's affect on others that is at the heart of the novel and that, ultimately, the reader too comes to experience. Few people leave this book without having been touched in some way by Einstein.

THEMATIC ISSUES

One specific issue raised by *Watchers* is the repeated use of Mickey Mouse as a motif. Einstein loves watching Mickey Mouse videos, and requests them for a Christmas present. When Nora and Travis are searching for names for the child they will have, Einstein suggests that it be named Mickey or Minnie. Einstein's own first litter of puppies is christened Mickey, Donald, Daisy, Huey, Dewey, and Louie. The Outsider is also entranced by Mickey. When Lem Johnson find its lair, he sees on the shelf of special objects that The Outsider has collected a Mickey Mouse coin bank, and he is reminded of one of the lab experiments run at Banodyne to determine Einstein and The Outsider's ability to distinguish between fantasy and reality. A videotape of film clips of everything from documentaries to *Star Wars* to Mickey Mouse cartoons was shown to them, and both learned to distinguish fantasy from reality, but "the one fantasy they most wanted to believe in, the fantasy they clung to the longest, was Mickey Mouse. They were enthralled by Mickey's adventures with his cartoon friends" (265–66). And when The Outsider is severely wounded, waiting to die, it is holding a Mickey Mouse video that it has taken from Einstein. Almost its last words are "Mickey," and then it asks Travis to kill it—something Travis does as a final mercy to a creature that should never have been born.

These scenes with reference to Mickey are at first funny and touching, and then, at the end, very sad. They carry a weight within the work that seems to suggest they are intended as more than a charming detail— that Mickey Mouse represents something fundamental to the novel's worldview—and it is striking that, in fact, Mickey Mouse has something in common with Einstein and The Outsider: all three are creatures created by human beings to serve the needs of human beings.

Mickey is, of course, a fantasy who does not even bear much resemblance to a real mouse. Einstein appears to be a golden retriever, but really is a genetically engineered animal who only looks like the rest of his breed. And The Outsider, although initially bred from a baboon, is intended to be hideous, to look like no other living creature. Designed to accompany men into battle, it has been engineered to be doubly effective as a weapon, since its monstrous appearance will create terror in those it hunts and kills.

We are given three types of pseudo-animal: one a fantasy, one who can survive only by disguising his true nature, and one who cannot survive because of its true nature. Only one of these man-made animals is a success in its own right, and that is the fantasy animal—the mouse who has brought delight to children all over the world. Perhaps the underlying message here is that human beings are not really meant to manipulate other creatures, that only in the world of fantasy can we be creators of successful alternative lives. Or perhaps, more ominously, the message is that unlike Einstein and The Outsider, human beings are not capable of differentiating between fantasy and reality. As a consequence, we bring great pain and sorrow into the world by continually trying to make our fantasies into realities. In this reading, the irony of Mickey Mouse is that the dog and The Outsider, who love this icon of childhood, are in fact more adult than the humans who have developed them, since they have the maturity to understand fantasy for what it is; by virtue of this understanding, they know that human beings can successfully create other creatures only in the world of fantasy, not in the world of reality.

The underlying theme of *Watchers* is that happy childhoods are only a fantasy; they exist only in the world of Mickey Mouse. In the world of reality, no one can make us happy. Instead, we must achieve our own happiness, and we can do this only by caring for one another, by watching over one another. When reading the novel, the reader is struck over and over again by images of a childhood that cannot be recaptured, and that was in fact flawed to begin with. The novel opens with a scene of Travis attempting to recapture a pleasure from his childhood—the shooting of rattlesnakes—but he cannot do so; when he finds a rattlesnake, he cannot pull the trigger. And he has taken with him on his journey the food of childhood—Oreo cookies and Kool-Aid—but only the cookies taste good to him; the Kool-Aid is far too sweet. On examination, perhaps it is as well that he cannot go back to his childhood since, with all its deaths, it held far more pain than pleasure. Surely this is a flawed childhood; every child should have a family and no child should have to endure repeated deaths.

Nora too has an aberrant background, one in which she has been frozen in an artificial childhood. Raised by an embittered aunt, she has been kept at home all of her life, isolated on the pretense that she is too sickly to attend school and must be educated at home, where the aunt can keep her in perpetual childhood. This is a flawed childhood also, one based on the dishonest manipulation of a child by the adult responsible for her. Einstein and The Outsider are also in a sense children, in their case of the scientists who have developed them and who intend, like Nora's aunt, to keep them in a state of perpetual childhood—that is, perpetually under their control—in laboratory cages.

Each of these characters achieves self-realization by setting aside the constraints imposed by such childhoods. Travis decides not to accept the pattern that loving someone means the death of that person, Nora decides not to accept the message that safety lies in reclusiveness, Einstein and The Outsider decide to escape the lab and take their chances in a world where they will always be other. In doing so, each arrives at self-realization and peace of a sort. Travis and Nora fall in love and create a family, Einstein combines satisfactorily the world of dog and the world of super dog, and The Outsider achieves its own death, with the strong possibility that it has overcome its biological limitations by developing a quality of mercy and even humaneness that it was supposedly bred to be incapable of developing.

Thus, all of these characters have achieved successful resolutions to their lives despite the childhoods they have endured. Nora tells Einstein that we all have the duty to help one another arrive at such resolution, that "we are watchers, all of us, watchers guarding against the darkness" (419) and the gift that we have to offer one another is that of love. This is the message that Einstein has brought to everyone he has had contact with, and it has changed them all, helping them free themselves from the harms of childhood.

ALTERNATIVE READING:
THE WRITER'S TECHNIQUES

One of the delights of analyzing fiction is that doing so can help the reader understand how the magician has performed the trick, how an author has gone about creating a work that has unity and is a pleasing whole. In literary analysis, the term unity refers to a work having "some organizing principle to which all its parts are related. . . . A work with *unity* is cohesive in its parts, complete, self-contained and integrated" (Holman and Harmon 1992, 489). The critic M. H. Abrams (1971) expands on this definition, seeing a work as an artistic whole when all of the plot elements are directed toward an intended effect and none of them can be omitted without seriously imbalancing the whole. The concept of unity originates with Aristotle's discussion of unity of action, by which he means a story plotted in such a way that everything in the work contributes to its resolution; there are no loose ends, no paths that lead to blank walls. In popular literature, some of the best examples of unity are found in mystery and detective fiction, especially in the Golden Age (1920–1930s) novels of authors like Agatha Christie. In a work such as *The Murder of Roger Ackroyd*, Christie develops a story in which everything, from physical items to visits by outsiders, contributes to the solution of the murder and at the conclusion readers are left with no unexplained clues or unanswered questions.

As a general rule, it is relatively easy to achieve unity in a work that focuses on one story line, but progressively more difficult to do so as other story lines are introduced. In this case, the writer must juggle all the subplots so that by novel's end, all are resolved. Characters must be balanced so that when the novel closes, everyone's fate is known. Readers must be given markers for connecting the many different threads of the novel, so that they are always aware of where they are in the story, of what is happening to whom, and of why it is significant. Often, one element or another of this mix is overlooked so that the reader ends the work unclear as to what has happened to X or what is the final outcome of Y. But in *Watchers*, Koontz performs a fine juggling act, one that he maintains for 483 pages. He does this by centering all plot strands, characters, settings, and the theme itself on one issue—the hunt for Einstein. This hunt serves the same function as the hunt for the killer in *The Murder of Roger Ackroyd*. Each of the many subplots in *Watchers* is in some way focused on Einstein: Travis's state of mind is the rationale for his first meeting with Einstein; the rapist's attack on Nora is the rationale for her first meeting with Einstein; the victims of the contract killer have been selected because of their work in developing Einstein; The Outsider is defined by his relationship to Einstein; the high-tech world of computer hacking creates false identities so that Nora and Travis can hide Einstein. Each of the settings in California—the Santa Ana Mountains, San Francisco, Big Sur, the Pacific Ocean, the countryside near Carmel—

is in some way integral to the task of keeping Einstein out of the laboratory. And the NSA, the government agency charged with tracking Einstein down, is prevented from doing so by one of its own agents because of his need to protect Einstein.

There are a number of patterns and themes in *Watchers* that appear in other Dean Koontz novels. Killers who kill for the joy of it and who have very high metabolisms, along with dainty consideration for what is hygenic and socially correct, appear in many of his works (see *Mr. Murder*, 1993). Computer hacking is becoming a staple for him (see *Midnight*, 1989). Women who take responsibility for their own fates are frequent characters (see *Whispers*, 1980). Much detail on guns and security systems, all of it carefully researched, is an almost expected aspect of a Dean Koontz novel. The sense that society as a whole is dangerous and that the individual can survive only by finding an isolated spot is common (see *Mr. Murder*, 1993). Federal agencies that blindly follow rules and regulations without regard to their impact on the individual is a frequent theme (see *Strangers*, 1986). Lonely childhoods in which the caretakers act with little care appear in many works (see *Cold Fire*, 1991). Genetic engineering, biological mutations, and extrasensory perception all play roles (see *Bad Place*, 1990). In fact, even the love of Disney characters appears in works besides *Watchers* (see *Dragon Tears*, 1993).

What is unique about *Watchers*, though, is the seamlessness with which its many elements fit into a unified whole. At the conclusion of the novel, all the plot lines are resolved, and readers' expectations are fully satisfied. Evil has, at least temporarily, been contained with the deaths of the scientists responsible for Einstein and The Outsider, the destruction of all records outlining the means by which they were created, the death of the contract killer and The Outsider, the closing of the file on the government search for Einstein, and the successful new life established by Nora, Travis, and Einstein.

This is a very optimistic ending. It reinforces the theme that by watching out for one another, by being responsible for ourselves and for each other, it is possible to achieve a good life. There is a great sense of peace in the novel's closing scene, when Einstein asks Nora if his pups will remember him and she answers, "As long as there are dogs and as long as there are people fit to walk with them, they will all remember you" (483). Koontz's achievement in this work is such that we might reword the ending to say that as long as there are Dean Koontz readers, a dog named Einstein will be remembered.

Lightning
(1988)

Nearly all of Dean Koontz's later novels are stories of suspense, a broad category covering works that include elements of many different genres and that has as its defining characteristic the fact that "the characters and the reader are in a constant state of uneasy anticipation of the worst, which all too often happens" (Rosenberg and Herald 1991, 47). However, Koontz's early novels were science fiction tales and he has continued to use certain conventions of that genre in his later novels, giving depth and richness to the individual works. A good example of this is *Lightning* (1988), whose premise is based on time travel and the possibility of alternate histories.

GENRE

Of all Dean Koontz's recent novels, *Lightning* is the easiest to characterize, since it follows the conventions of the science fiction subgenre of alternate worlds, in which a story looks at the possibility of alterations in history and considers what the world would be like if X had happened instead of Y, and the conventions of the closely related subgenre of time travel, in which a character or characters travel into the past, the future, or both. In *Lightning*, time travel is limited to going into the future, with the characters who do so specifically attempting to alter the course of history by their actions.

PLOT DEVELOPMENT

Plots can usually be divided into four parts, the original situation, the complications, the crisis or climax, and the denouement; for definitions of these terms, see Chapter 3. In *Lightning*, the original situation is that a child is about to be born into the world and about to undergo all of the experiences that fate has in store for her. She is Laura Shane, and she will be the central character of the novel.

The initial complication in the novel is the appearance of a stranger at the house of the doctor who is scheduled to deliver Laura. Although his colleagues at the hospital do not know this, the doctor has become a very heavy drinker and on the evening Laura will be born, he is drunk. Holding the doctor at gunpoint, the stranger calls the hospital and tells them that the doctor is drunk and will not be able to deliver the baby. Another doctor takes over and Laura is born healthy and sound, but her mother dies in childbirth. Subsequently we learn that if the original doctor had delivered Laura, he would have bungled the birth in such a way that her spinal cord would have been severely damaged and she would have spent all of her life in a wheelchair.

The intervention of the stranger sets the pattern for the novel as a whole: as Laura grows up, she is faced with life-threatening situations in which the stranger, who she comes to think of as her guardian angel, intervenes. The next event occurs when she is eight years old and a drug-crazed gunman holds up her father's corner grocery store, intending to rape the little girl as well as take the money. The stranger bursts in, kills the gunman, concocts a story for Laura's father to tell the police, and then disappears. She next sees the stranger when she is twelve years old and at her father's funeral. The stranger is there but does not talk to Laura, although she recognizes him from the events in the grocery store. He disappears as suddenly as he came, but a new character also appears here, a man dressed all in black who stares at Laura and asks her, "Why you?" She has no idea what the question means, but her impression of him is that he is evil. Like the guardian angel, he too disappears.

Complications continue building when Laura, now an orphan, is sent to a children's home. Here she meets the Ackerson twins, Ruth and Thelma. They are identical, very intelligent and very funny, and they become Laura's closest friends. In the home she is stalked by a pedophile who, if fate is allowed to play out its course, will repeatedly rape and beat her. The guardian angel appears to the pedophile and beats him up, warning him away from Laura, but this backfires and the pedophile becomes determined to get revenge for the beating on the girl. Shortly after, Laura is taken in as a foster child by two kind, loving people who cannot have children of their own. It now seems that she may have a happy life after all, but the pedophile follows her to her new home and attacks her there. In trying to get away from him Laura stabs him with the base of a broken glass. The shards go into his throat and he dies. The foster mother enters the house, sees blood all over the place, a dead man, and a terrified girl; has a heart attack; and dies on the spot. Laura goes back to the home, where she rooms with the Ackerson girls again and Tammy, a very quiet, depressed girl who has been sexually abused by both her father and, later, the pedophile attendant in the home.

When Laura turns thirteen, she is moved to a home for older children. Here, she learns that there has been a fire at her old home, and that two children were killed. She has a premonition that the two were Thelma and Ruth, but in fact they turn out to be Ruth and Tammy. Tammy, who had attempted suicide earlier, has immolated herself with lighter fluid and in the ensuing fire, Ruth is killed before Thelma can get to her. Thelma is moved to the home for older children, and she and Laura live there together until they are eighteen, forming the only family each has now. When they leave the home Thelma begins what will eventually be a career as a very successful comic, and Laura, helped by a small trust fund from her father, goes to college, where she majors in creative writing. She meets Danny, a very nice, sweet man who adores her. He's a stockbroker and a good one. He and Laura fall in love and marry, and Laura starts writing novels. She is published almost immediately, and each succeeding book she writes is more successful than the last. Danny quits his job to manage her career and they have a son, Chris. They are told that he will be their only child—Laura can have no more children.

At this point, the guardian angel intervenes in Laura's life once again, when she, Danny, and Chris are scheduled to be in a horrifying traffic accident on a hilly, icy road in a snowstorm. Their car will be hit by an out-of-control vehicle driven by a drunk and they will all die. Because the guardian angel forestalls this, all three survive, but then the man who appeared at the funeral dressed all in black appears again and opens fire on the three of them and Danny is killed. Thus, where fate intended that three people would die, two survive and fate is cheated again. The guardian angel helps Laura concoct a story about a drug feud that they were inadvertently caught up in (since no one is likely to believe that a guardian angel appeared out of nowhere to save Chris and Laura), and he warns Laura to be on guard at all times because people will come for her. As a result she masters the use of various weapons and always has one with her.

The guardian angel is identified as Stefan Krieger, an SS man working at a place referred to only as "the institute," which is set in Berlin in 1944, just before the end of the Second World War and the defeat of Nazi Germany. The institute has developed a time travel machine, the Lightning Road. It can send people forward in time but not back, and so the researchers at the institute go into the future to find out what happened at the end of the Third Reich, and what they can do to change the ordained outcome, the defeat of Hitler's Germany. Krieger comes from a family loyal to Hitler, but he is now thoroughly disillusioned, recognizing the Third Reich for the brutalizing dictatorship that it is. On one of his journeys into the future he sees Laura as fate intended her to be—in a wheelchair, autographing her new novel—and he falls in love with her. This is the catalyst that brings about his first intervention in her life, when he goes forward in time to see to it that she is not maimed when she is in the process of being born.

The researchers at the institute, in their attempts to guarantee that Germany will win the war, are particularly interested in collecting enough information on atomic weapons for Germany to be able to complete its own. One of these researchers, Kokoschka, who is head of security at the institute, becomes curious about Stefan's many trips into the future and his interest in Laura. How can she possibly relate to the war and the future of Germany? He follows Stefan and appears to Laura as the man all in black, who seemed evil. Once Kokoschka realizes that Laura has no role in the fate of the Third Reich, he shoots Stefan, having discovered that Stefan is a traitor. Stefan in turn kills Kokoschka and returns to the institute to destroy it, but discovers that he is too late and that his plan will not work. He returns to Laura, still wounded, just before a group of Gestapo hit men arrive to kill Laura, Stefan, and Chris. Laura kills them, takes Stefan to a doctor, and then the three of them go into hiding, with the help of Thelma, who is now very successful and very wealthy.

In the climax, Stefan goes back to Berlin to destroy the institute so that no one can go into the future and make Germany the victor in the war. While he is there he also appears to both Churchill and Hitler, assuring that on the one hand the institute will be destroyed by precision bombing and, on the other, that Hitler will suspect nothing and will think everything is going as planned regarding time travel and the saving of his regime. At the same time, another group of hit men, a squad of the SS, come for Laura. They trap her in the desert and in the ensuing shootout Chris is killed and Laura's spinal cord is severed, in both cases reinstituting what was originally ordained by fate: Laura was to have spent her life in a wheelchair, and there would have been no Chris in her life. Stefan comes back to the desert just after Chris is killed and Laura wounded, and through manipulations of time travel, sends a message in a bottle to Laura just before the SS attack so that she and Chris can run away and save themselves. The forewarned Laura is then able to kill all the SS men, saving Chris and herself.

Finally, in the denouement Stefan initially lives with Thelma and her husband, who shelter him until Laura can get him documentation that will give him a new identity and allow him to live safely in 1989. At the end of the novel, Laura has fallen in love with Stefan, Thelma is expecting twins, and all are living happily ever after. We also learn that because Stefan had warned Churchill that Stalin would, at the end of the war, create a dictatorship in Russia and Eastern Europe, Churchill has arranged that Stalin's regime be destroyed by the Allies. At the end of the story, people are casually commenting about how the losers in wars seem to benefit a good deal from their defeats, talking about how Germany, Russia, and Japan have become postwar industrial and economic success stories. Thus, besides changing Laura's fate, the fate of all of Russia and Eastern Europe has been changed.

One specific issue raised by *Lightning* is the horrible death by fire of Ruth Ackerson when she is only twelve. The other deaths in the book are, in one way or another, both acceptable and necessary for the story: it is the death of Laura's mother that introduces Stefan and his mission of saving Laura from the fate that was ordained for her. It is the death of Laura's father that makes her an orphan and becomes the rationale for her subsequent life in foster homes and the state children's homes, where she develops both her ability to endure and the imaginative world that will eventually make a writer of her. The death of Danny gives her the rationale for becoming a fighter and it also fulfills part of her destiny, since she was never intended by fate to know and marry Danny. All the rest of the deaths, with the exception of Ruth, are those of people who are evil in one way or another, such as the SS and Gestapo men, the drug addict who attempts to rape a little girl, the pedophile Willy Sheener who preys on the children in the home, and so on. These are people whose deaths are mourned by no reader.

The death of Ruth Ackerson, though, is death of another order. She is only twelve years old, and she is all the family Thelma has. The two girls were orphaned when they were nine and have been living in a home for the last three years, since it is difficult to find adoptive parents for children of their age, and finding them for a set of identical twins determined to stay together makes it even harder. Like many identical twins, Ruth and Thelma complement one another, seeming to be more together than each is alone, and they play off one another in clever, witty ways, with Ruth as the kinder, wiser sister, and Thelma as the wise-cracking cynic.

When Ruth dies, it is in a manner that is consistent with the good person she is. Ten-year-old Tammy Hinsen, a pitiful girl who has been sexually abused and who rooms with the Ackersons, has attempted to commit suicide in the past. She does so again and this time she succeeds, setting fire to herself with lighter fluid as she lays in bed. The fire flares up and Thelma breaks out the windows so they can escape. She turns to reach for Ruth, but Ruth has backed into the room, trying to smother the fire burning Tammy by throwing her blanket over the girl. Instead, Ruth herself catches fire and before Thelma can grab her, the room explodes into flames. Thelma, who cannot reach Ruth, goes out the window. Eventually she comes to accept Ruth's death and the fact that she could do nothing to save her. Life becomes good again for Thelma, "but never the same as it had been before the fire" (87). There is no plot necessity for having Ruth die—she does not enter into the drama of time travel and of Laura's guardian angel attempting to change Laura's fate— and her death is difficult for the reader to accept.

A useful way to approach an issue such as this, one that raises a question and poses no obvious answer, is to ask what would happen if the event were handled differently—to consider how this might change the work. If, for example, Ruth did not die, what effect would that have on the story? Perhaps Laura and Thelma would not become as close as they do, since part of their bonding is their joint mourning for Ruth; but as they are close anyway, this seems a weak reason for having Ruth die. Thelma's humor, the basis of her success as an adult, would probably not be as effective as it is, since the death of Ruth and the experience of her loss add a tragic undertone to Thelma's comedy; but again, this seems an insufficient reason for the death of a child.

However, Ruth's death does bring about another change in Thelma who, along with mourning Ruth, also comes to celebrate her, to think of all the good things in her life as in some way a testament to Ruth and to her love for Ruth. She assures Laura that Ruth would have approved of Danny, that she would have found him perfect for Laura. When Laura tells Thelma that she is putting her into one of her books, Thelma makes certain that Ruth will be in it, too. Thelma shares her own pleasure in the fact that she is carrying twins with Ruth, thinking what pleasure they would give her. Ruth seems always to exist in Thelma's memory and, in this way, to share in her happiness. If, then, Laura learns through her experiences in the novel first to endure, then to fight, and then to accept, Thelma takes the sequence one step further by going beyond acceptance and celebrating the love that she and her sister had (and in her memory, still have) for one another. In this, she becomes a model for Laura, and thus the plot rationale for Ruth's death is that it will provide a pattern whereby Laura, the protagonist of the novel, can attain peace.

CHARACTER DEVELOPMENT

The major character in *Lightning* is its protagonist, Laura Shane, the orphan who has been taken under the wing of a man from the past who acts as her guardian angel. Laura is a well-rounded character, since we know a good deal about her. Koontz has described her background, her relationship to her father, her experiences after her father's death, her friendships, her love for her husband and child, and her profession. She is also self-defined as a dynamic character, since she tells the reader that she has changed, that as a child, "I learned to endure. After Danny was killed, I learned to fight. Now I'm still an endurer and a fighter—but I've also learned to accept. Fate *is*" (354). This is a subtle change: as a child, Laura fought back and killed a pedophile—no enduring here— and we certainly know that she will fight for herself, for her son, and for anyone who is dear to her. In terms of enduring, it is difficult to see what the difference is between that and accepting fate; surely both are a form of endurance, of putting up with that which one cannot alter. At the beginning of the novel she is a brave, imaginative, self-reliant person, and at the end of the novel these qualities still define her. The one change that is evident in her is that her definition of love has broadened to include a man besides Danny since she has come to love Stefan, something she believed would never be possible for her.

Lightning's other major character is the protagonist Stefan Krieger, who is flat (nondimensional) and static (unchanging), even though he plays such a large role in the novel. Very little of Krieger's background is filled out, except for the fact that his father was an early member of Hitler's inner group. This is the rationale that gives credibility to Stefan's membership in the SS—he joined when he was too young to realize exactly what it represented—and for Hitler's trust in him. It also explains why he would have a very sensitive job in the institute. However, little more than this is given of his background, and although he says that the horrors he has taken part in as a member of the SS are what has turned him against it, the reader must take this on faith: none of these are shown, nor do we see him arriving at new insights concerning himself and the world around him. It is also never clear why Laura is so important to him that he returns over and over again to the future to protect her, although he says that it is because of the strength and beauty he sees in her face, even though she is in a wheelchair, and the power of her novels, all of which he has read. Since the reader never knows the Laura he's referring to—the one who was crippled at birth—and since we do not have the chance to read Laura's novels, the basis for the attraction must, like the SS experiences, be taken on faith. Like Laura, Stefan is a static character: at the beginning of the novel his goals are to protect Laura and destroy the institute and, with it, the chance that Germany might win the war. At the end of the novel, he has achieved both. What he may now become, a character from 1944 living in the world of 1989, is left to be developed in another novel.

The third protagonist of the novel is Thelma Ackerson. She is funny, witty, and dear, and she plays a larger role in the story than the number of lines given to her would suggest. Little is explained about her background before entering the children's home, but the interplay between Thelma and her sister Ruth, and their acceptance of Laura, creates the sense of a family and hence of a background. Their advice to Laura about what to do if she finds herself in a foster home that she can't stand is funny and credible, and feels exactly right for two twelve-year-olds who've been through the foster-child mill: "Ruth said, 'Just weep a lot and let everyone know how unhappy you are. If you can't weep, pretend to.' 'Sulk,' Thelma advised. 'Be clumsy. Accidentally break a dish each time you've got to wash them. Make a nuisance of yourself' " (57). And when Laura finds herself in such a home, the Ackerson techniques work. Later, when Ruth dies in the fire, Thelma's despair feels very real and we see her as a dynamic character—someone who has come to learn that the tragedies in life stay with us, and if we are lucky, they become one part of our total experience rather than dominating it. It is interesting that the loss she feels for Ruth is far more moving than is any other character's reaction to loss in the novel: Laura's father to the death of her mother in childbirth, Laura to her father's death and later, to her husband's. This is a function of the fact that Thelma's loss is always with her, that Ruth always exists for her in her present life rather than in the distant past of her childhood. At the very end of the novel, when she is talking with Laura about the fact that she might be carrying twins, she says, "Think how pleased Ruthie would be for me" (354). Thelma is an excellent example of Koontz's ability to flesh out a minor character in such a way that the character takes on life for the reader.

He does something similar with the character of one of his antagonists, the pedophile Willy Sheener, known to the girls in the home as the White Eel. He is a physically ugly man—Koontz's description of him makes him sound like a perverted Howdy Doody—and he seeks out the weak, lonely, unsure girls in the home, giving them candy bars and Tootsie Rolls in exchange for sex. He seems the epitome of evil until Stefan, in his role as guardian angel, breaks into Willy's home to wait for him. He enters his bedroom and discovers that it is a child's room, with bunny rabbit sheets on the narrow bed and furniture built to a child's scale. Sheener also has children's picture books and toys in his room, and they are clearly his, there for his own pleasure and not for some child he might bring there. It seems to Stefan that "Sheener molested children not solely or even primarily for the sexual thrill of it but to absorb their youth, to become young again like them" (61). With this brief description, Koontz takes a character who would otherwise be a stock character—the stereotypical dirty old man who lures children with candy—and he makes something more of him, a person who is tormented and in his torment, forever seeking that which he will never have. Sheener is, however, a static character, since he does not gain insight into himself or the reasons for his actions; he doesn't live long enough for this to take place.

The major antagonist in the novel is Heinrich Kokoschka, a member of the Gestapo and head of institute security. He is a fine example of a stock character, since all we know of him is that he is the classic villain: he is thoroughly evil, he tells Laura that he likes to kill, and when she first sees him, she thinks, "Wintery darkness was an integral part of the man himself" (37). He is so complete a bad guy that he even dresses in all black, and as soon as we read his description, we know his role—one that he never deviates from. There is virtually no background information on Kokoschka, and like all stock characters, he ends as he began, in his case evil to the core.

A final character who is also a stock character is Laura's eight-year-old son, Chris. Thelma always calls him "Christopher Robin" after the classic owner of Winnie the Pooh and Piglet, and he could in fact be Christopher Robin or Timmy of *Lassie* fame or any other spunky young boy who is brave, sensitive, knowledgeable, and loving. Chris has a splendid scene in which, because of all the time he's spent watching *Star Trek*, he is able to explain the paradoxes and limits of time travel to his mother. Other than this, he is every brave young boy who has adventured through the pages of innumerable children's books and here he is, adventuring once again.

SETTING

In Dean Koontz's works the country often serves as an outpost or retreat to which characters withdraw for the safety that they hope distance and isolation will provide and that they sometimes do provide, depending on the novel. The country is used in precisely this way in *Lightning* when, after the death of Danny, Laura takes Chris and retreats to her house in the San Bernardino Mountains. It is far from any other home and is set almost in the middle of thirty acres of land, so that anyone approaching is visible long before the person reaches the house. Here, Laura can set up a firing range and learn to handle weapons without endangering neighbors or raising questions. She keeps Chris at home with her, having him specially tutored in the house rather than going off to school, where he would be vulnerable to others. Eventually, she is attacked at this retreat, but not before it has fulfilled its function of providing her with a safe place in which to learn the techniques of self-defense.

Other than the mountain retreat, Koontz does not do a great deal with homes and buildings in *Lightning*, with the exception of the pitiful child's bedroom that he creates for Willy Sheener. However, he makes very effective use of clothing to help establish Thelma Ackerson's character. When she appears in Laura's wedding as her witness, Thelma has her hair in a strange, spiky, multicolored style and is wearing tight black pants, a black shirt with artfully arranged holes all over it, a heavy chain belt, and red high heels. She also has on an earring that seems to be a fishhook. She explains to Laura that it's the punk look, popular in Britain but so far unknown in the States, and that it's the perfect look for her: "It's great for my act. I look freaky, so people want to laugh as soon as I step on the stage. It's also good for *me*.... [with punk] you get to hide behind flamboyant makeup and hair, so no one can tell just how homely you are" (105). The style exactly fits Thelma's personality: it's attention grabbing and audacious, and it also reflects her insecurity about her looks. (Apparently, when the Lord gave Thelma and Ruth intelligence, wit, and bravery, He decided that was sufficient, and moved on to others to hand out handsomeness and beauty.)

The most dramatic use of setting in *Lightning* is the phenomenon that gives the book its title. There are extraordinary lightning storms here, used to herald the arrival of someone who has come through the time tunnel—maybe Stefan, maybe one of the Gestapo squad, maybe SS hit men. The first use is typical of how lightning will be used throughout the novel. It occurs when Stefan is coming to stop the doctor who would otherwise deliver Laura and bungle the birth. There is a tremendous thunderclap that seems to come from the sky and the ground simultaneously, "as if heaven and earth were splitting open.... Two extended, overlapping, brilliant bolts seared the darkness.... A chain of thunderbolts made the front lawn and street appear to jump repeatedly.... All color was burned out of the night" (5–6).

POINT OF VIEW

In *Lightning*, Koontz uses the third-person omniscient point of view, in which an unknown narrator who can see into the minds of all the characters tells the story and includes the thoughts of many people. This point of view is very well suited to this story, since it enables Koontz to show, from one central, coherent point of view, Stefan Krieger in 1944 Berlin, Laura Shane in 1989 California, and the many characters who move in and out of different time frames. This gives the novel unity and enables the reader to track where and when the action is taking place, an important consideration when a writer is dealing with something as complex as time travel and the limitations put upon events by the paradoxes time travel imposes. With this point of view, we can watch Kokoschka watch Stefan, who is in turn watching Laura, and be clear about who is doing what and where we are in the exposition of the story. It is difficult to imagine the story told from another point of view. For example, first person would not work here; we would see only from the perspective of one character and the story line demands that we know what Stefan sees in Willy's room and, at the same time, know how Laura feels about her foster family. Stefan cannot feel what Laura feels, nor can she see what he sees, but the use of third-person omniscient allows the reader to perform both of these feats.

THEMATIC ISSUES

When reading *Lightning*, one is struck by the references to fate as an active agent, a force that determines our lives through a series of causes over which we have no control. The term fate as it is used in the novel refers to a programmed pattern imposed from without on human life. Thus, when Laura, who has been saved from being raped by the drugged gunman who broke into her father's store, is threatened in the children's home by Willy Sheener, Krieger thinks that perhaps this is her fate, that if he saves her from one rapist, another is bound to appear at some later point in her life. And when Laura is running from the hit men she thinks that there is a particular spot on a road that she must not return to, that if it had not been for Stefan's intervention she and Chris would have died at that spot and if they go back, they will die now because "fate strove to reassert predetermined designs" (191).

In discussing the events that happened to Laura when she was a child, and whether or not some of them could have been avoided, Stefan tells her that is it very possible that they could not have been, since "Destiny struggles to reassert the pattern that was meant to be" (251). However, in the denouement this statement is amended somewhat when Laura, again thinking about destiny imposing a pattern, thinks, "But sometimes, happily, it fails" in the attempt. And on the next page she amends this again by thinking, when she learns that Thelma is to have twins, "And sometimes, happily, it succeeds" (354). She then has the discussion with Thelma about how she has come to accept fate, not just endure it or fight it, and Koontz's underlying theme here is what it is that enables her to do this—what enables her, like Thelma, to celebrate what she felt for her father, for Danny, for Ruth. These are all people she has loved dearly, and they are people who have loved her dearly.

Hence, *Lightning*'s underlying message is that in loving one another, we give each other the courage to accept life and our individual fates. Koontz opens Part 1 of the novel with a quotation from the philosopher Lao Tzu: "Being deeply loved by someone/gives you strength;/while loving someone deeply/gives you courage" (1). It is this strength and courage that Thelma has gained through Ruth, and Laura through her father, Ruth, and Danny. Now, like Thelma, she can celebrate them and at the same time accept their fate and her own, recognizing the truth of Thelma's statement that human beings are a vulnerable species. As in many of his novels, Dean Koontz ends with the strong affirmation that it is our love for one another that makes life worth living. If we cannot control fate, we can at least control our reaction to it, and it is our love for one another that ultimately allows us to do this.

ALTERNATIVE READING:
A READER-RESPONSE ANALYSIS

Reader-response analysis is based on the concept that, to some extent, each of us reads a book differently because each of us responds to a particular work from our individual perspective. We bring to that work our backgrounds, our experiences, our education, our biases, our loves, and our hates; in doing so, we unconsciously emphasize or deemphasize certain aspects of the text. We each create our own text, and the book that I read may be quite different from the book that you read, even though we are both reading Dean Koontz's *Lightning*.

This, of course, raises the question of the value of doing any analysis at all, since a particular analysis may be valid only for a particular reader. In general, though, we share many of the same backgrounds and experiences, since we are members of the same culture and live in the same time period. Because of this, one person's analysis of a work is very likely to be similar—or at least acceptable—to that of a great many other readers. And coming from such a shared culture, it is also very likely that a particular analysis will shed light that will benefit other readers by helping them enlarge their perspectives on a work. If I see a work as emphasizing relationships between people and another critic sees the same story as emphasizing the constraints imposed on people by the society around them, perhaps each has had something to learn from the other; perhaps each of us, by reading the other, can broaden our sense of the novel we have read, and see more in it than either of us may have seen alone.

In doing a reader analysis, the critic consciously does a subjective analysis—one that is deliberately based on the critic's personal background—and readers understand that the reading is subjective. In my own case,

Lightning is one of my favorite Dean Koontz novels (my other two favorites are *Watchers* and *Dark Rivers of the Heart*), despite the fact that *Lightning* is, in terms of genre, a work of science fiction and I rarely read that particular genre. Nonetheless, this is the Koontz novel with which I identify most closely. The reasons that I do so have little to do with its time-travel and history-altering elements; instead, it is because of the two protagonists, Laura Shane and Thelma Ackerson.

Like Laura Shane, I can absolutely relate to the fantasy of having a guardian angel. I think it would be wonderful to have someone out there watching out just for me, ready to intercede when something terrible is about to happen. It certainly wouldn't hurt to have that someone be a tall, handsome, blue-eyed blond who just happened to recognize how special I was. In fact, as a child I envisioned my guardian angel as looking exactly like this, and my longing for such a creature in my life came surely in part from the fact that I was a brown-skinned minority and, on top of that, a female. As many different studies have shown, members of minority groups tend to be more fearful of the world at large than are members of the majority. We tend to see bias waiting around every corner, verbal slights and put-downs likely to drop from anyone's tongue, and an attitude of caution toward us from most people around us who are holding us in judgment, waiting for us to prove ourselves as worthwhile. Of course, it makes sense to see the world in this way if one is indeed likely to be facing such attitudes, and any person who is in a minority at some time does indeed face these attitudes, but it's also an exhausting way of looking at the world. It's hard to go through life always keeping one's guard up. For this reason, it would be grand to have a guardian angel—someone who could just step in and take over if things got out of hand.

It is also particularly difficult for a child to understand prejudice. I vividly remember thinking that I couldn't help the color of my skin, that it wasn't something I had deliberately chosen in order to offend the people around me, and that surely I should be judged only on those qualities that were within my control, like honesty, kindness, loyalty, and the like. At the time, it seemed almost supernatural to judge someone for something that God had done to them, and therefore it also seemed reasonable that God would provide an antidote. And what better form for an antidote to take than that of a guardian angel? His being tall, blond, handsome, and blue-eyed wouldn't hurt either, since the dominant culture in which I grew up was white Anglo-Saxon male, and if you're going to have a protector, have that protector come from the strongest group around. Thus, because of my own childhood, I am predisposed to accept a guardian angel who acts as a protector for a little girl subject to forces well beyond her control.

I also find that I identify not so much with Laura, the novel's protagonist, but with Thelma, a positive character but, with respect to Laura, a minor one. I suppose the reason that I don't identify with Laura is because she is beautiful, not a self-image I grew up with. By the same token, one of the reasons I do identify with Thelma is because she is so definitely not beautiful. There is even some suggestion that one of the reasons she and her sister Ruth were unlikely to be adopted was because of their looks: "Not pretty girls, they were astonishingly identical in their plainness: lusterless brown hair, myopic brown eyes, broad faces, blunt chins, wide mouths" (44). I read this and think that surely they were meant to be triplets instead of twins, with me as the third member. They substitute for good looks the qualities of intelligence, energy, and being good-natured—qualities far more within my grasp as a child than beauty. I also identify with their roles as outsiders. They are orphans, belonging to no established group, and although I was not an orphan, I was definitely an outsider by virtue of being a minority group member. There is also something very seductive in the notion of twinhood. Like many children, I was convinced that really I was a twin, only something had happened and someone had taken my twin away. And, of course, for Thelma there was such a person, until something happened and her twin was taken away.

I also find that I identify with Thelma as an adult in her role as struggling comic. Humor is a powerful survival tool—if we can laugh at something, we are less likely to cut our wrists over it—and it is also a powerful weapon. People are a bit careful, a little on their guard, when they are around someone with a quick sense of humor, because they never know when it might be turned against them, and no one wants to be laughed at. Therefore, if one feels at bay in the world, humor acts as a survival tool in this way. Finally, the way Thelma dresses has the same effect. In her punk clothes she is attracting attention to herself rather than hiding, hoping not to be noticed, and this is exactly what women are told to do to protect themselves. Over and over we hear that the way to become a victim is to look meek and mild, to hide, to avoid eye contact, to become mouselike. (Poor Tammy, the sexually abused child who commits suicide in *Lightning*, almost exactly fits this description.) Instead, we are told to walk tall, look sure of ourselves, and meet everyone's gaze with a direct gaze back. If the world is a dangerous place, one way to meet that danger is by looking strong, assertive, and daring—and that is exactly how Thelma looks in her garish punk clothes. There is also an innocence and naïvete to this: if only the right clothes would protect us, how much easier life would be. And when one thinks about the power of logos, of such figures as the polo player prominently displayed on Ralph Lauren clothes, it would seem that many of us do buy into this concept and believe that clothes will make us powerful and, by extension, safe.

Clearly, this is a subjective response to the topic of guardian angels and the character of Thelma, and it is likely that few other readers will respond in this particular way. Nonetheless, such a response is both valid and useful because it can help readers to see a side of Thelma that they may not have thought about; in doing so, they will find more in the story than if they were limited to their own subjective responses. The danger in such subjective readings is that one's reaction to the story, or to some minor element in the story, may be so strong as to seriously distort the work. But this is unlikely to happen if readers analyze their own subjective readings and think about why they have reacted to a work as they have. In doing so, they will not only enrich their experience of the work but also gain self-knowledge, and that's as good a reason for reading a book as anyone has ever come up with.

Midnight
(1989)

One intriguing aspect of studying the work of Dean Koontz is that of genre. Koontz himself considers his work to fit into the suspense genre, but most critics think of him as a writer of horror fiction, and he is usually grouped with such horror writers as Stephen King, Peter Straub, Robert McCammon, and John Saul. In the totality of Koontz's work, the suspense classification is in fact the most accurate (see Chapter 2), but for specific novels the horror classification is equally appropriate, and it is easy to understand how Koontz came to be labeled a horror writer.

A good example of a work that would seem to place Koontz firmly within the horror genre is the novel *Darkfall* (1984). In this story Baba Lavelle, a voodoo priest who has dedicated himself to the black arts, is seeking revenge on a New York City Mafia family for the death of his brother. The brother was a crime reporter and had done an uncomfortably accurate series on drug running in the city, and on the people responsible for it, and so the crime lords had him killed. Now the voodoo priest is seeking to kill them in return, using as his weapon minor demons that he calls up from hell. When the police set up a task force to investigate the weird series of deaths in which various members of the mob have been sliced, torn, and gnawed to death by animals that cannot be identified (and cannot be stopped with bullets), Detectives Jack Dawson and Rebecca Chandler are named as its heads. Lavelle calls Dawson and explains to him that he and Dawson have the same goal, the eradication of drug pushers, gamblers, pimps, murderers, and the like, and therefore Dawson should call off the investigation. Dawson explains that he cannot do this, that he cannot condone the killing outside the law of anyone, even if that person does belong to the mob. Lavelle then says that if Dawson does not cooperate, he will kill Dawson's two children, eleven-year-old Penny and seven-year-old Davey.

At this point, Dawson goes to a Houngon, a practitioner of white magic in the voodoo rights, for information and help. The Houngon tells Dawson that he will be safe, that he is a righteous man and that evil spirits do not have the power to kill a righteous person. However, the protection does not extend to his children: while they are innocent, they have not yet proven themselves to be righteous. Grotesque creatures from hell begin tracking the children—in their bedroom, at their school, and later in a car. Dawson and the Houngan work to close the gates of hell and deny the creatures access to this world, and Chandler takes the children into a cathedral for protection, where they huddle before the altar while the creatures watch them, perched on the altar rail. When Dawson succeeds in his mission, the creatures turn to clumps of dirt and the children are saved.

On the surface, then, this is a scary story involving the supernatural and demons from hell, but there are more than superficial reasons for considering it a good example of horror. In *The Penguin Dictionary of Literary Terms and Literary Theory* (1991), J. A. Cuddon says that in the hands of "a serious and genuinely imaginative writer the horror story . . . explores the limits of what people are capable of doing and experiencing," and certainly Koontz does this in his terrifying descriptions of the attacks of the creatures on the children and of the physical extremes that Dawson, Chandler, and the Houngan go to in order to save them. Cuddon also says that the good horror writer works within the areas of "psychological chaos, emotional wastelands, psychic trauma, abysses opened up by the imagination," all of which also apply to the character of Baba Lavelle who, as a result of the murder of his brother, is in psychological chaos, is living in an emotional wasteland, has suffered a psychic trauma, and is literally calling up creatures from the abyss to assuage his intense grief. Cuddon further describes the horror story as one that "explores the capacity for experiencing fear, hysteria and madness, all that lies on the dark side of the mind and the near side of barbarism," and again, this description applies to *Darkfall*, a large part of whose terror lies in the extreme fear of the monster-stalked children. Finally, Cuddon sees such stories as representing "various kinds of hell—taking 'hell' to be a more or less universal symbol of an extreme condition" such as "intense grief . . . irredeemable loss, acute fear, irrational foreboding or physical pain" (417). This is a work where not only the antagonist Lavelle but also the protagonist Dawson and the two innocent victims, the children, are living in the hell of intense grief—Lavelle because of the loss of his brother and Dawson and the children because of the death of his wife and their mother. The latter is a death with which, throughout the course of the novel, all three finally come to terms after having suffered fear, foreboding, and pain. Thus, although there are elements of the police procedural and the love story in *Darkfall*, the focus of the novel is on the terrors of the psychological and the supernatural; for this reason, it is indeed accurate to place *Darkfall* in the horror genre.

Alternatively, a work such as *Cold Fire* (1991), which on the surface also seems to be a conventional horror story and, as such, helps to explain Koontz's reputation as a writer of horror, is on examination best categorized as a work of science fiction. Its unifying plot device is that of parapsychology and its horrors are specifically seen as emanating from the mind of one person rather than from the gates of hell. Thus, *Cold Fire* focuses on the horrors created by individual mortals rather than on those that are supernatural. In doing so, it suggests that all horror is ultimately capable of being understood and, therefore, controlled.

Unlike most Dean Koontz novels, *Cold Fire* has very few characters, and of these, only two are significant, the protagonists Holly Thorne and Jim Ironheart. Jim considers himself to be the agent of a higher power, either God or some supreme being. This power warns Jim ahead of time when certain people are going to be killed so that he can intervene and save them. Holly Thorne, a reporter for an Oregon newspaper, witnesses one of the rescues and starts researching Ironheart, who will give no interviews and withholds even his name. She finds that he has saved a number of people across the country, and that there seems to be little pattern to who is rescued: they are of different ages, incomes, professions, and so on. Just as she is about to confront Ironheart at his home, she sees him leave very quickly and assumes that he is setting out on another mission. Following him, she ends up on an airplane a few seats behind Ironheart. He recognizes her from Oregon and tells her that the plane will crash and hundreds will be killed. It does indeed crash, but through Thorne's persuasion and Ironheart's intervention, most of the people are saved. Characteristically, Ironheart disappears again, but Thorne follows him back to California and confronts him there, asking him how he knows when someone is in danger and why he helps some people and not others. How does he choose who will be saved? He tells her that he doesn't know, that a voice tells him where to go and, once there, who to save.

As this is going on Thorne begins to have nightmares in which she is in a windmill and evil creatures are oozing through the walls with the intent of killing her; at the same time, Ironheart has similar dreams. He believes the origin of the dreams is something he calls The Enemy, a 10,000-year-old alien that lives in a deep pond next to a windmill on the farm he grew up on.

So far, we are very much in the world of horror, especially with creatures coming out of walls in old, deserted mills. But as it turns out, there are no creatures—they are only the projections of Jim Ironheart's mind. As a young child he demonstrated psychic powers. His parents formed a stage show around him in which he would take objects from people in the audience, hold them, and then tell the owners something about themselves. When Ironheart was ten years old his parents were killed in a shoot-out in a restaurant, and he was the only survivor. He went to live with his grandparents on the farm with the windmill, and handled his grief—as well as the feeling that he should have been able to stop the killer, maybe by freezing the trigger on his weapon, maybe by mentally forcing him to drop it—by retreating into a fantasy world based on ancient creatures living at the bottom of the pond. A year later his grandmother was killed, breaking her neck in the mill, and when his grandfather blamed him for her death, Ironheart retreated even further into his fantasy.

Some twenty-five years after these events, Holly Thorne helps Ironheart to see that there are no creatures out there, that "The Enemy is the embodiment of your rage over the deaths of your parents. Your fury was so great, at ten, it terrified you, so you pushed it outside yourself, into this other identity. But you're a unique victim of multiple-personality syndrome because your power allows you to create physical existences for your other identities" (350). Instead of just creating other personalities that live only in his mind, Jim can actually project them as physical phenomena, as nonhuman entities.

Once he accepts that this is the source of his and Holly's terrifying dreams, Ironheart is a whole person, a single personality. And because he still has his paranormal powers he can continue to save people, only now he has Holly to help him. Together, they are a sort of psychic Superperson and Assistant Superperson (Holly specifically rejects the role of Lois Lane; she wants a more active role than that of recorder of some-one else's brave deeds). In terms of genre, then, the novel best fits the science fiction subgenre that focuses on stories of extrasensory percep-tion. This is a branch of soft science fiction, a term that refers to stories based on the social sciences of psychology, sociology, anthropology, and the like, as opposed to the hard sciences of physics, chemistry, biology, and so on. In *Cold Fire* the explanation for the demons is psychological, and their physical appearance is based on the fact that Jim Ironheart has extrasensory perception: he has precognition, since he knows what will happen before it actually happens, and he also has the powers of clair-voyance and telekinesis. Basically, this novel investigates what would happen if a person who had a split personality also had paranormal powers, and it is therefore a projection of a known soft science, that of psychology, mixed with a classic staple of science fiction, the positing of the existence, at least in some people, of extrasensory perception.

Where the novel *Darkfall* creates a good case for considering Koontz to be a writer of horror stories, and *Cold Fire* contains enough elements of that genre to at least make it understandable that critics would con-tinue to see him in this way, a novel such as *Midnight* (1989) shows that the horror category is an oversimplification when applied to Koontz's work as a whole. His writing is too complex in terms of the conventions he uses to be conveniently placed in any single genre. *Midnight* is an excellent example of such complexity. It is a mystery, and it opens with one of the classic mystery devices: was a suicide really a suicide, or was it murder? It is a technothriller in its careful descriptions of weaponry and computers. It is a horror story in its descriptions of human beings taken over by predators. It is a science fiction story in its exploration of the theme of cyborgs. It is a love story in the development of the rela-tionship between Sam Booker and Tessa Lockland, the major protago-nists. And like *Watchers* (1987) and *Dragon Tears* (1993), it also features a wonderful dog, making it an animal story, too.

PLOT DEVELOPMENT

In *Midnight*, the original situation (the world of the work of fiction before something happens to disrupt it) is that a resident of the small, peaceful town of Moonlight Cove is out for her usual evening run along the beach—something she does every night at this time and has been doing for years. The initial complication is that someone or something follows the runner and attacks her, killing her. The police then report the death to her mother, who lives in another town, as a suicide, and convince the mother that the body should be cremated. The mother and sister are suspicious: it seems very unlikely to them that the victim would have committed suicide, and they wonder about the police chief's insistance that the body be cremated. The sister, Tessa Lockland, decides to go to Moonlight Cove to clear up the victim's effects and see what she can learn about her death.

At the same time, other mysterious deaths have occurred in Moonlight Cove, those of a trio of union workers who supposedly died in a car accident. Their bodies have also been cremated, and the FBI have come in to investigate because the deaths may be related to the victims' union activities and therefore may be an infringement of their civil rights. The FBI agents learn nothing, but they feel that there is some sort of conspiracy going on in the town on the part of the police and the citizenry to see to it that the FBI is pacified and, at the same time, is given no information. This causes yet a further complication, when the FBI agents obligingly leave but send in an undercover agent to find out what is really going on in Moonlight Cove.

Complications increase further when a young girl, Chrissie Foster, witnesses something terrifying about her parents (her assumption is that they have been taken over by aliens) and is locked into a pantry by them for hours, until she can be "converted." It then turns out that conversions, whatever they may be, are taking place all over Moonlight Cove and that some of those who are converted regress to a primitive state where they become predators who prowl the surrounding area, delighting in the hunt and the kill. At first these regressions are seen as an aberration, but it soon becomes apparent that more and more of the "converteds" are regressives and that they cannot change back into human form. Chrissie escapes from her once-parents and there is a hunt to find and convert her before she can report what she has seen. At the same time, Tessa Lockland is nearly attacked in her motel and escapes to a laundromat to wait for daylight, where she meets Sam Booker, the undercover agent. Booker arrived in town only to discover that his presence and agency affiliation are known to the police, who mount a search for him and for Lockland. Booker has been sent into town as the result of a letter to the FBI from a Moonlight Cove resident, Harry Talbot, a disabled Vietnam veteran. In the letter Talbot alleges that something very strange is going on in Moonlight Cove and that it involves the police and all those in positions of power. Booker and Lockland go to Talbot's house for sanctuary while they figure out what to do and eventually, they are joined there by Chrissie Foster, who succeeds in escaping her hunters and chooses Talbot as a last resort, since everyone else in town seems to be in league with her parents and the police.

When this group is all together they are able, because of what each has seen, to piece together what must be happening in Moonlight Cove: Booker has the FBI reports and has broken into the police computer files, where things are definitely not right for a town of this size (the police have sufficient computer access to run a small country, and this is a town of only 3,000). He learns through doing this that all of the police computers are linked to the main computer at New Wave Microtechnology, a cutting-edge computer firm that employs most of the people in the town. Foster has seen the physical changes in her parents and, later, in her priest, and has heard discussion of the "conversions" and of the need to convert her. Lockland has heard the attacks in the motel and has seen one of the attackers. And Talbot, who is confined to a wheelchair and who partakes of the life of the town by observing it through his telescope, has seen a large number of bodies—at least twenty—taken into the funeral home and cremated. In some cases, he has seen the state of the bodies, terribly torn and ravaged, as if by a powerful, vicious animal. The four of them decide that something is being done to change people, that it involves everyone in the town including all the members of the power structure, and that it is centered at New Wave. They work out a plan to communicate with the FBI offices, and Foster, Lockland, and Booker leave to carry it out, with an armed Talbot waiting to fend off the converters who are scheduled to come for him that evening.

In the climax, Thomas Shaddack, the owner of New Wave Microtechnology, discovers through his computer hookup what Booker is doing in the high school and goes there to confront and kill him so that Shaddack's plans for converting the entire town, a prelude to converting the entire world, can continue. Loman Watkins, the town's chief of police, makes the same discovery about Booker through his computer hookup and, realizing that Shaddack will be at the high school, goes there to confront and kill him in order to stop the conversions. Shaddack takes Tessa and Chrissie hostage but is killed by Watkins, instantaneously causing the deaths of all the converted in Moonlight Cove. This also saves Harry Talbot, since he was on the verge of being killed by one of the converted who died in the split second before he would have succeeded.

Finally, in the denouement the reader learns that Tessa, Sam, and

Chrissie Foster will form the nucleus of a new family that will include Sam's alienated son Scott who, it is strongly suggested, will no longer be alienated, and that Harry and his dog Moose will join the family in the near future. As to what will happen to the peaceful little town of Moonlight Cove, each reader is left to draw his or her own conclusion.

CHARACTER DEVELOPMENT

Midnight's protagonists are Sam Booker, Tessa Lockland, Chrissie Foster, Harry Talbot, Loman Watkins, and Moose, a dog trained as a Canine Companion. Booker is a round or fully developed character, since we know a good deal about his background and the influences that have shaped him. His mother died in a car accident when he was seven and he then went to live with his father, an alcoholic and a child abuser. He served in Vietnam and then became an FBI agent. He has had six close brushes with death including one near-death experience, his wife died very painfully of cancer, and he has a poor relationship with his sixteen-year-old son, Scott. When he enumerates his reasons for living, they are bleak and depressing: Guinness stout, really good Mexican food, Goldie Hawn (he actually means his fantasy of Goldie Hawn, since he has never met her), and his fear of death. He works as an undercover agent because he is a loner who avoids close relationships. He is one of only two characters who are dynamic. At the end of the novel, Booker comes to understand that he is afraid of living rather than afraid of dying and, as a result of this insight, he is able to say, "Now, I'm *eager* to live again" (450). He returns to his son, Scott, determined to establish a relationship with him based on love, and the reader believes that he will succeed in doing this.

Tessa Lockland, sister of one of the first victims of the regressives, is also a well-rounded character. We know of her relationship to her mother and sister, and why she has come to the town. A gutsy, intelligent woman, she is blonde, petite, and beautiful, and so is usually assumed to be a bimbo. By profession she is a maker of film documentaries and, therefore, she is accustomed to dealing in facts, a background that helps her confront what is happening in Moonlight Cove. Like Booker, she has come close to death—in her case during her filming of revolutions and uprisings throughout the world. But unlike Booker, her experiences have added to her positive outlook on life, making her appreciative of being alive to experience a new day tomorrow. She is a static character, ending the novel with the same insights and perceptions as she began it.

Chrissie Foster, the eleven-year-old attempting to escape her parents and the converters, is also a well-rounded character. We have a good sense of how she feels about her parents, herself, her situation, and how she views the world. She is typical of many of Koontz's young women characters (see, for example, the Ackerson twins and Laura Shane of *Lightning*, discussed in Chapter 6) in that she is brave, resourceful, and funny. In some ways she could be considered a stock character, since Foster conforms to a type found repeatedly in literature—the prepubescent girl who, at least for this time in her life, enjoys the prerogatives of being a boy, prerogatives that open the world of adventure to her. However, Foster's fantasy life—in which she envisions herself as an author commenting on, shaping, and forming her experience—takes her outside of the bounds of stereotype and makes her a self-motivating character. Like Lockland she is static, since she ends the story as the same bright, positive, life-affirming person that she began it, despite the horrors she has been through.

Harry Talbot, the disabled Vietnam veteran who takes in Booker, Lockland, and Foster, is also a well-rounded character, although he plays a smaller role in the novel than do the other three. The characteristic that most distinguishes him is his response to his disability. His use of the dog Moose as his assistant is fondly and imaginatively described, so that we are able to understand, without having to be directly told by the author, what a source of companionship and even humor Moose is to him. The description of how Talbot uses his telescope in order to feel a part of the life of the town is equally imaginatively described, so that it is seen as a tool that makes him feel part of the community rather than something that makes him a nasty man spying on his neighbors. Like Lockland and Foster, Talbot is also a static character, ending the novel with the same strong affirmation of life as he began it.

Loman Watkins, the town police chief, is a character who begins as an antagonist, but at novel's end becomes a protagonist. He is a flat character in that all we know of him is his reaction to the events in Moonlight Cove, but by the same token, he is a dynamic character, since he begins the novel thoroughly approving of Shaddack's conversions and ends it in absolute disgust, recognizing that Shaddack has destroyed the humanity of the residents. An agent of law and order, he himself becomes a murderer, killing not only Shaddack but others who have been monstrously changed by the conversions, including his eighteen-year-old son,

Denny, whom he loves (or did love, when Watkins could still feel emotions other than fear).

The novel's final protagonist is the dog Moose, a service dog who has been trained by the real-life group Canine Companions for Independence, described by Koontz as "a nonprofit organization that provides its furry assistants at nominal cost to those who need them. All dogs give us love and loyalty, but *these* splendid animals give even more than usual: they literally transform the lives of the disabled people with whom they are paired, serving as their arms or legs or eyes or ears, and allowing them to venture into the world with confidence" (471). Koontz invites readers to make a contribution to this organization, and his description of Moose, a brave dog with, believe it or not, a sense of humor, will make anyone who gives to charities seriously consider donating to Canine Companions. As animals go Moose is a round character, since we know about his training, his priorities, and even his sense of fun, and he is a static character, ending the story with the same excellent qualities as he began it.

The novel has three antagonists: Thomas Shaddack, Running Deer, and, arguably, Sam Booker's son, Scott. Of these, the major character is Shaddack, an extraordinarily wealthy man who has developed a very successful, cutting-edge computer firm and is now using his wealth and expertise to put into place the Moonhawk Project, a plan dedicated to making humans and machines into cyborgs—that is, into one conjoined being. Shaddack is a well-rounded character in that his childhood background is given, making believable his adult actions. His motivations, his hopes and dreams, and those experiences that led him to become the person he is are sufficiently sketched. Although he is dominated by his lust for power, the source of the lust is clear, making Shaddack more than one-dimensional. He dies convinced of the rightness of the Moonhawk Project, gaining no insight into the horror he has brought upon the town, so he, too, is a static character.

Running Deer is an Indian who worked for Shaddack's parents and who has long been dead, appearing in the novel only as a vivid memory of Shaddack's. Running Deer seeks vengeance against Shaddack's father, a judge who let go the men who killed one of Running Deer's brothers and severely disabled a second. His instrument for this vengeance is to be the young Tom Shaddack. However, Running Deer's plan backfires: he succeeds in convincing the boy that he is a chosen person—someone who is beyond the normal moral confines of human beings—but when he then turns the boy on his parents, he is too successful. Tom kills both parents and does so in such a way that Running Deer is blamed for the deaths. In Shaddack's adult fantasies of Running Deer the character is dynamic, since he comes to the realization that what he did to the boy was wrong. However, this insight happens only in Shaddack's imagination and so, ultimately, Running Deer is static.

The final antagonist is Booker's sixteen-year-old son Scott, a sullen boy who is hostile, confrontational, and interested only in Satanic music. He is very much a stock character—the young person who escapes into a world of rock and roll and drugs rather than face reality—but there is some indication that he will be a dynamic character, since there seems at the end little chance that Scott will be able to resist the combined loving attentions of his father, Tessa Lockland, Chrissie Foster, Harry Talbot, and Moose. In fact, it is entirely possible that Moose the good service dog will help another disabled person besides Harry, the emotionally crippled Scott, which would then make Scott into another stock character, the boy brought to full humanity by his relationship with his dog. But that would be another story. . . .

SETTING

In *Midnight*, the setting is once again California, this time the northern coastal town of Moonlight Cove. But even though it is a small, isolated town, it does not provide the peace and security that we usually expect from such a place. Once it did so—once it was a place where a runner could run on the beach at 10 P.M. and not be afraid; once it was a place where there was only one violent death in ten years, and that was an automobile accident. Now there have been twelve deaths in three weeks, and the only person foolish enough to run on the beach at night is one of those found dead. Many of the stores in town are closed, and no one walks the streets anymore, even during the day.

Something is clearly wrong here, and the fact that it can be wrong in a place traditionally associated with everything going right—with rural, small-town America—makes the story that much more frightening: if something awful can happen here, then it can happen anywhere. The small-town setting also helps to make plausible the shutting off of the town to the outside world, since it is already an isolated place, bordered by ocean on one side, and therefore relatively easy to isolate. And finally, the size of the town adds to the plausibility of the cyborg experiment, since it would be far easier to "convert" people in a small, isolated place and keep the process secret than it would in a major city, since in a small town people know and trust one another. They will give one another the benefit of the doubt and will be unlikely to turn to outsiders if they have questions about what is going on.

Koontz makes good use of the weather to add to the sense of something mysterious, unseen or only half seen, in the town of Moonlight Cove. He emphasizes the fog that drifts through the town in tendrils, hiding and distorting what is there, making the characters always a little uncertain about what they have actually seen. The fog works as both a benefactor and a malefactor, doing good when it hides a protagonist such as Chrissie Foster from the view of the forces who are hunting her down, but doing evil when it covers up the predatory movements of the regressives. In this way, it adds to the mystery of the novel, since the reader never knows when the presence of fog signals good or evil and thus never knows when to relax, when to be tense and alert.

An inspired use of setting in *Midnight* is that of the architecture of the houses. The most detailed descriptions are those of Thomas Shaddack's house and Harry Talbot's. Both are radical, hi-tech, modern designs, emphasizing that the people who live in them are something other than the fishermen and surfers one might expect to find in a California coastal town. They are instead a bit out of the ordinary in their interests and tastes. The patterning of the two ultra-modern buildings—one the site of the source of evil in the novel, the other acting as a safe house or sanctuary for the protagonists—emphasizes the dual uses of modern technology. This is a technology that brings with it the promise of ultimate good and ultimate evil. Through its wise use, humans may be able to live almost forever; through its unwise use, humans may be eradicated from the face of the earth.

POINT OF VIEW

In nearly all of his works, Dean Koontz uses the third-person omniscient point of view, in which an unknown narrator who can see into the minds of all the characters tells the story and includes the thoughts of many people. This is very effectively used in *Midnight*, since this point of view allows the reader to follow the novel's many subplots. Will Tessa Lockland escape from whoever is tracking her in the motel? Will Sam Booker be able to communicate with his bureau? Will Chrissie Foster escape her parents and those who are stalking her? Will Harry Talbot escape the converters? Will Loman Watkins locate Thomas Shaddack before Watkins regresses? Can Thomas Shaddack be stopped? Third-person omniscient allows the reader to shift from one story to another and still keep track of the overall picture, since the narrator is able to switch with ease from one plot line to another.

It is difficult to imagine another point of view working as well for this particular novel. First person would not work, since it would give the point of view of only one character, and the reader would know only what that character knew. Third-person limited is a possible choice, but would be difficult to follow, since the reader would be seeing the events from one person's point of view, then shifting to another's, then to another's, then to another's. Usually, third-person limited is reserved for one character because of the difficulty of keeping the reader on track when there are shifts in point of view. One other possibility is that of third-person dramatic, in which an unknown narrator tells readers what is happening, but does not allow the reader to become privy to any of the character's thoughts. This point of view would be an ideal choice for Harry Talbot, since he can only observe and make his deductions on the basis of what he sees; he cannot get into the minds of those he watches. However, if Harry were chosen as the novel's voice, much would have to be left out, since his vision, while greater than that of the average resident in Moonlight Cove, is necessarily limited to what he can see through his telescope. If it isn't in his field of vision, he cannot describe it for the reader, and so he could not see Foster locked in the pantry, Lockland in her motel room, and Booker in a patrol car. We would lose these strands of the plot until the denouement, when all suspense would be over and they could not add to our fear. Thus, third-person omniscient is both the most efficient and the most effective choice for telling the story of *Midnight*.

THEMATIC ISSUES

The theme of a work is rarely specifically stated. Instead, it must be discovered by analysis. However, *Midnight*, like Koontz's novel *The Bad Place* (see Chapter 8), is an exception to this general rule. In these two novels theme is made explicit, perhaps because Koontz wants to be very sure that readers understand the specific points he is making in each novel.

Koontz builds to his theme through his discussion of the two different types of change experienced by the characters who are converted, emphasizing that these are changes they themselves bring about. Because the conversion process leaves them unable to bear their existence as emotionless human beings, some become regressives and revert to primitive, predatory animal states where existence is based almost solely on emotion. Other converteds change in a different way, becoming more machinelike rather than more animallike. They physically attach their organs to their computers, sharing circuitry between human and machine, so that there is no longer a clear dividing line between what is human, what is machine. Loman Watkins finds his son Denny attached to his computer by "metallic cords, in which the boy's fingers ended, [that] vibrated continuously and sometimes throbbed as if irregular pulses of thick, inhuman blood were passing through them, cycling between organic and inorganic portions of the mechanism" (307).

When Watkins, remembering the boy his son once was, kills the creature he has become by shooting him, the computer screen fills with the message "NO NO NO NO NO NO NO" and Watkins realizes that the boy is only partly dead, that "the part of the boy's mind that had inhabited his body was extinguished, but another fragment of his consciousness still lived somehow within the computer, kept alive in silicon instead of brain tissue." Now the screen flashes the message, "WHERE'S THE REST OF ME WHERE'S THE REST OF ME WHERE'S THE REST OF ME NO NO NO NO NO NO NO NO"(312). Sam Booker, trying to find a computer that will give him access to the outside world, comes across people like Denny who have melded with their computers, and he realizes that there is a term for them, that such a person is a "cyborg: a person whose physiological functioning was aided by or dependent on a mechanical or electronic device" (335) such as a pacemaker or a kidney dialysis machine.

Clearly, there are some very good reasons for humans to become dependent on machines, but such dependancy can also be abused, as it has been for the characters who have melded with their computers. Booker sums this up when he says, "The greatest problem of our age . . . is how to keep technological progress accelerating, how to use it to improve the quality of life—without being overwhelmed by it" (347). He, Lockland, and Talbot then discuss the fact that machines hold great attraction for human beings, that a part of us wants them to take over our functions, make our decisions for us, be responsible for us. After all, Thomas Shaddack really believed that his conversion project was for the benefit of mankind, that people would have better lives if they could live logically and rationally, free from the turmoil of their emotions. Talbot wonders if perhaps humans should not meddle with the natural order. Booker says that since machines can be used to benefit mankind, we have to try to use them in this way.

Realistically there is no going back to a premachine age. The theme of the book is that we must become responsible for our own inventions and we must hope that we can keep them out of the hands of people like Thomas Shaddack. The novel's message is an equivocal one: Koontz's protagonist says that humans must try to contain and control their own inventions, but he makes no promise that we will be able to do so.

ALTERNATIVE READING: DECONSTRUCTION

One type of literary analysis is that of deconstruction, in which a work is looked at from the perspective of the many possible meanings of the text. This method of analysis derives from the theories of the French philosopher Jacques Derrida, who shows "that a text . . . can be read as saying something quite different from what it appears to be saying," that "it may be read as carrying a plurality of significance or as saying many different things which are fundamentally at variance with, contradictory to and subversive of what may be . . . seen by criticism as a single, stable 'meaning' " (Cuddon 1991, 223). Steven Lynn (1994) gives an excellent example of such fluidity of meaning by describing a sign placed next to an elevator. The sign reads, "Seeing Eye Dogs Only." Most of us would assume that what this meant was that only blind people accompanied by seeing eye dogs could use this elevator, but what it actually says is that only seeing eye dogs can use the elevator: their human owners must use the stairs or some other elevator, and certainly no other animals can take this car. Lynn says, "Here's a text ostensibly put up to help blind persons, and it actually ignores them. A blind person with a seeing eye monkey, presumably, must not ride. Plus, blind persons obviously cannot read the sign, which suggests that some other intention does motivate it." He lists a number of other possible interpretations and then asks, "What *is* the point of this sign?" (90).

Well, what *is* its point? Most people reading it would assume that it was intended for sighted people, to warn them that the elevator was reserved for blind people accompanied by seeing eye dogs, and they would also assume that somewhere along the way, some sighted person would point out to blind persons that there was an elevator just for them and their dogs, and that this was it. However, while we might all agree that this is a reasonable interpretation, we would surely also have to agree that the sign can be read in other ways, as Lynn has so read it. And while it may seem that Lynn's reading is extreme—that no one would actually read the sign in this way, that everyone really knows what it means—such ambiguities of language are with us constantly. We simply overlook them as mistakes or errors to be quickly forgotten, since we have been conditioned to consider them as getting in the way of "real" meaning. Some wonderful examples of alternative meanings can be found in the responses of nonnative speakers to a second language. (I once had a Vietnamese student say to me, "I know what the verb 'to use' means—I *use* a pencil for writing, a typewriter for typing—but what does it mean when someone says 'I used to live in Seattle?' ").

Also, there are examples of alternative meanings in the questions of children. One of my children, at about the age of seven, asked me what was wrong with us. I said, "There's nothing wrong with us, honey."

"Well," he said, "what's different about us?"

I said, "Different how? What makes you think we're different?"

And he said, "Well, why do we wear size Irregular?"

It's a funny story, and it is also a fine example of the mutability of meaning: if clothes are marked small, medium, and large, meaning that they are for small, medium, and large-sized people, and if one group of clothes has stamped over such markings one that says irregular, why shouldn't this group be for irregular-sized people? And if we pursue this, are queen-sized clothes really only for queens? Can I buy my baby a toddler size if my baby is not yet toddling? And what on earth is meant by a petite size 16? Is this for large petite people? And if it is, what *is* a large petite person?

Of course, as a general rule language really isn't as ambiguous as the examples quoted suggest. Most of the time, it is used by people who mutually understand the context and therefore are in agreement on its meaning. But for people who love language, deliberate misinterpretations or misreadings are fun. On a more serious level, they can reveal meanings that are in contradiction to the intention of the writer or speaker. This does not mean that the writer or speaker is secretly undermining the message, but rather that all messages are to some extent ambiguous; by recognizing this ambiguity, we gain a deeper perception of the possibilities of language.

In analyzing *Midnight*, a deconstructionist critic might explore the theme that human beings are incapable of forming sustaining bonds, whether in the natural or in the man-made world, since no one in the novel has what is usually thought of as normal family life. Sam Booker, for example, is a widower with one child, from whom he is estranged. His parents were divorced when he was young, and so he has effectively had only one parent—first his mother and then, on her death, his alcoholic father. He is an only child. Tessa Lockland has lost both her father and her sister, and has only her mother left, a mother who cannot come to Moonlight Cove to help her because she is recovering from a broken leg and so can be defined as an absent parent. Tessa is now an only child, since she had only the one sister. Chrissie Foster has lost her parents, since they have devolved into predators and are no longer human. She too is an only child. Harry Talbot has no family, since both of his parents are dead and he is apparently an only child. At least, no mention is made of any siblings in discussing Harry and his isolation. Loman Watkins has one child, Denny, whom he kills when Denny becomes a cyborg. Although there is one scene with Watkins's wife, she seems to have left the family subsequent to being converted, since Watkins does not consult her when he decides to kill Denny, nor does she appear in any subsequent scenes. Thomas Shaddack is also an only child whose parents had almost no relationship with him as he was growing up, leaving him in the care of servants. When the story takes place he is an orphan, since he has killed both his parents. He had a surrogate parent in the form of the Indian Running Deer, whom he also killed. He has not married, nor does he have any children.

In sum, then, in the world of *Midnight* no one has what we would ordinarily think of as a family, with mother and father, brothers and sisters, uncles and aunts, grandmothers and grandfathers. Instead, the characters have at best one family member, with whom they have either a long-distance relationship (Tessa Lockland) or are in conflict (Sam Booker). A usual literary interpretation of these incomplete family structures would be to look at them in the context of what they say about life in contemporary America, and to point out that they describe a society marked by the breakdown of the traditional family and, by implication, of traditional values and moral standards. However, another way of interpreting the structures would be to see them as pointing out the essential impossibility of creating relationships that will sustain us over time. It can't be done biologically, since no one here has succeeded in doing it, and furthermore, relationships with machines break down too—the humans in *Midnight* either revert to animals or become machines themselves.

Thus, a deconstructionist analysis emphasizes the essential loneliness of human beings—creatures doomed to be born and to die alone—and points out that such a state is a tragic one, since we try over and over again to establish relationships that are ultimately denied us by our very natures. In such a reading the novel's ending emphasizes the work's underlying tragic worldview: we are doomed to attempt to create that which it is beyond our means to create, and we see this when Sam Booker goes home, hoping to reconcile with his son Scott by taking with him an entirely new family for Scott, a family that will have a mother (Tessa Lockland), a sister (Chrissie Foster), an uncle (Harry Talbot), and even a family dog (Moose). This may seem an optimistic ending, but the deconstructionist would point out that it is in fact pessimistic. At the close of the work Scott has no mother, no sister, no uncle, not even a dog, nor does he give any evidence of welcoming these. For him to accept this ersatz family would be to change his nature, as it has been described in the novel.

However, since a deconstructive interpretation can include many possible interpretations, the novel does not have to be read pessimistically. On the basis of the text's internal evidence, the reader can just as easily conclude that Koontz's point is that the emotional needs of human beings can be met only by other humans. If our society has changed in such a way that the traditional family is no longer available to us, we must go out and create other families to take their place. Since the novel ends with the major characters setting out to do just this, the ending is optimistic. Its message is that human beings can take responsiblity for themselves and, one way or another, can create the relationships they need in order to have happy, meaningful lives—and even the attempt to do so brings fulfillment. Thus, in deconstructing the text of *Midnight* the reader can read it in two opposed ways, one pessimistic, one optimistic. And as to which interpretation is the correct one, a good deconstructionist knows that the word *correct* is just as ambiguous as any interpretation it might be applied to, and therefore there is no need to be concerned with correctness.

The Bad Place
(1990)

It is characteristic of Dean Koontz to introduce certain elements in one novel and then develop them further in subsequent novels, as though he wanted to look at them from other perspectives. Good examples appear in 1990's *The Bad Place*, in which Koontz created variations on character, plot, and setting from his 1976 novel, *Night Chills*, and also from his 1980 novel, *Whispers*.

The earliest novel, *Night Chills*, has a straightforward story line. A powerful and wealthy CEO, a corrupt Pentagon general, and an amoral scientist have joined together to test a new drug developed by the scientist that, when taken, makes its subjects highly sensitive to messages delivered through subliminal perception. They are now field-testing it in the small Maine town of Black River, by introducing the drug into the town's water system and sending subliminal messages via the cable television system that serves the town (the system is conveniently owned by the CEO). The effects of the drug are permanent, and it has only one side effect: when subjects are first given it, they have nightmares and wake up sweating heavily, and hence the title, *Night Chills*. If the field test is successful, the three villains or antagonists plan to use the drug to gain great power through mind control and eventually take over the world. Complications arise when a veterinarian and his two children come to Black River for their annual summer vacation, and they learn that almost everyone in town has just had the flu, complete with night sweats and bad dreams, with the exception of the owner of the general store and his daughter.

Readers familiar with science fiction already know that the veterinarian and the general store owner will figure out what is going on in the town and somehow foil the antagonists. Suspense in the novel is based on when the protagonists or heroes will discover what is happening, how they will stop it, and how much damage will be done before they stop it. There is never any doubt in the minds of readers that they will succeed, since doing so is a convention of this genre and Koontz's readers know that he will fulfill their expectations. The novel as a whole is plot-driven rather than character-driven, holding the reader's attention by making the reader want to know what will happen next, rather than by engrossing the reader in particular characters and their development. However, one small role that is intriguing and stays with a reader long after the book is finished is that of Buddy Pellineri, an assistant night watchman at the mill in Black River. He is mildly retarded, perceives the world around him through images rather than words, and has a phobia about cats. In him Koontz has created a prototype for Thomas in *The Bad Place*, a beautifully drawn character who has Down's syndrome.

Besides drawing on *Night Chills*, *The Bad Place* makes use of an element first introduced in *Whispers*, a novel of identical-twin villains who are the result of an incestuous relationship forced on a young girl by her father. The father dies during the girl's pregnancy, and she goes away to have her baby, telling everyone in the community that she is staying with a friend who is about to have a baby and that she will be adopting the friend's baby and bringing it home with her. When the one baby turns out to be two, she clings to her first story and throughout their childhood treats the twins, both named Bruno, as one person, convincing them that they are aspects of one personality. Koontz's skill as a writer is such that he makes this believable to the reader. At least for the duration of the book, we accept the concept that two children could be raised as one, and that the community could be kept unaware of the fact that the one child was actually twins.

The mother also convinces the children that they are children of Satan and that the demon's sign marks their genitals. Because of this, they can never have sex (they interpret this to mean that when they do have sex, they must afterward kill the woman involved). Her technique for controlling the children is a behaviorist one, in which punishment is used to ensure a particular pattern of behavior. In the case of the young boys, this punishment consists of locking them in an underground root cellar full of giant cockroaches whenever they make any move to act as separate individuals. The title of the book comes from the whispery sound of all the roaches moving in the cellar. The mother tells the children that she will watch over them all of their lives, even after she has died, and that she will have the power to punish them even then, should they disobey her. She convinces them that she will return from the dead by assuming the bodies of living women. As a result, the adult twins (still acting as one and still one person to the world) seek out and kill young women who look like their mother, believing that she has taken over the women's bodies.

As a whole, *Whispers* is one of Koontz's weaker books. The reader figures out long before the characters in the novel do that the villain must be identical twins, and one of these obtuse characters is a trained police detective, who should be much better at deduction than any amateur reader. But again the novel introduces elements that will be explored in more detail in *The Bad Place*—children who are victims of incest; mothers who are convinced that their children are agents of God or Satan and have in turn convinced the children of this; pairs of identical twins; cats as symbols of evil; and even the effect of rustling insects on those who are terrified of them.

GENRE

The Bad Place is a good example of Koontz's cross-genre work. It combines science fiction in its use of teleporting and telepathy, mystery in the protagonists' attempts to discover the identity of a character suffering from amnesia, romance in the relationship between the major protagonists, and adventure because of its breathless chase scenes, both intercontinental and extraterrestrial. There are also elements of the horror genre in the vampirelike antagonist. However, he is not a true vampire, since he is not one of the dead who leave their graves and prowl in the dark of night; instead he is a human being who has been taught that he has a need for human blood. This gives the story elements of the psychological suspense novel, a subcategory of the thriller.

PLOT DEVELOPMENT

In *The Bad Place*, the original situation—that is, the world of the work of fiction before something happens to disrupt it—is really three sit-

uations, since the novel is composed of three subplots that run simultaneously and only begin to come together in Chapter 25 of this
57-chapter novel. In the first plot, the story begins with a man lying in
an alley. He is slowly coming to consciousness and although he knows
his name is Frank Pollard, the only other thing he knows about himself
is that he is afraid and that he is running away from something. He has
a flight bag with him, and all his instincts tell him to get away from
where he is. He steals a car by hot-wiring it (although he doesn't know
how he knows how to do this) and drives off, only to be followed by
flashes of blue fire that destroy the car. He runs from the car, manages
to elude the blue fire by hiding out in a condemned apartment building,
then steals another car and drives as far away as he can, up the California
coast. We subsequently learn that this dramatic scene is an accurate re-
flection of the man's usual situation, that he has been on the run for the
last seven years.

Meanwhile, the second subplot opens in Chapter 2. Julie and Bobby
Dakota are the happily married owners of Dakota & Dakota Investigations, a firm that specializes in industrial espionage. They are on a stakeout at a computer software firm, where a supposed security guard who
is actually a brilliant hacker is in the process of stealing a brand-new,
unreleased software program. The firm has discovered who the guard
really is, and Julie and Bobby are there to catch him in the act of stealing.
However, the guard is also aware that the firm knows about him, and
has arranged to have hit men kill the watchers as soon as he has completed copying the program. Since the guard has spotted only Bobby,
the hit men go just for his van. Julie, who is parked in a different area,
is able to rescue Bobby by killing the hit men, driving into one with her
car and spraying the other with automatic fire from her Uzi. She and
Bobby call in the police who arrest the hacker, and another case is successfully concluded for Dakota & Dakota. Julie and Bobby go home to
get some sleep before taking on their next case.

The events in plot one, focusing on Frank Pollard, alternate with the
events in plot two, focusing on Julie and Bobby's stakeout of Decodyne,
for the first twelve chapters of the book. Then Chapter 13 introduces the
third subplot with the scene of a man named Candy prowling silently
in a house with a sleeping woman and her two teenage children. Candy
attacks them one by one, taking them by surprise as they sleep in their
beds, and kills them by first knocking them unconscious and then drain-
ing the blood from their necks with deep bites into their carotid and
jugular veins. It is evident that Candy has been killing people in this

way for years, and we learn that he was taught to do so by his beloved mother.

The initial complication in the Frank Pollard subplot is that once he has escaped and hidden out in a motel where he can at last get some sleep, he wakes to find clear evidence that he has been somewhere and done something in his sleep—his face is scratched and his hands and shirt are covered with blood—but he has no recollection of where he has gone or of what has happened. In despair, he decides to consult a private detective because he is afraid to go to the police for fear of what he might find out about himself and also for fear that they just won't believe him. He goes to Dakota & Dakota and, in doing so, links the subplots. After some hesitation, Julie and Bobby take on Frank's case and set out to discover who he is.

They begin the search by putting him in a hospital for a series of tests to be certain that the amnesia is not the result of illness. Frank passes all the tests and then, in his bed in a private room with one of the Dakota & Dakota operatives guarding him, he disappears while the operative is watching. He then reappears and disappears in rapid succession. Subsequently the reader learns that Frank has the ability to teleport, although he has no control over the act; it is something his subconscious does when his survival is threatened. Again, Frank has no idea of where he goes or what he does when he teleports, but he always returns exhausted. This situation is getting progressively worse, and he is afraid that if it continues, he may not be able to return from wherever it is he goes.

At this point Julie and Bobby call in a friend of theirs, the hypnotist Jackie Jaxx, to see if he can put Frank in a trance and find out who he is and what it is that so badly frightens him. Jaxx succeeds, but Frank is so terrified that he teleports even while in the trance. Since Bobby is holding on to him at the time, Bobby teleports along with him. Through Bobby, we see where Frank goes and who it is that is following him. At this point, the third subplot is integrated into the main plot, since Frank's nemesis is Candy, who is Frank's brother. Frank killed their evil mother seven years earlier and Candy, who adored her, is seeking vengeance. When Bobby finally returns to Dakota & Dakota, he brings with him enough information so that Candy can be traced and matters brought to some sort of conclusion. However, just as Bobby has seen Candy, so has Candy seen him, and he now hunts Bobby in order to find Frank.

Another element of the plot adds to the complications in the person of Thomas, Julie's twenty-year-old brother, who has Down's syndrome.

Thomas adores Julie and is very sensitive to anything concerning her. He senses that she is in danger and sends his mind out to search for it, at which point he locates Candy, The Bad Thing. Thomas understands that Candy means death for Julie, and so he continues to mentally track him, although he is afraid to do so. He does not know that Candy can sense the mental presence of Thomas and is just waiting until Thomas feels safe so that Candy can trap him in a mental web and find Julie (and subsequently, Frank) through him.

In trying to learn more about Frank's background, and so protect him from Candy, Julie and Bobby track down Dr. Fogarty, the doctor who delivered the brothers. They learn from him that Frank and Candy and their identical twin sisters are the product of incest and inbreeding. Their mother was the child of a brother and sister pair, and was born a hermaphrodite. She had a very rare form of hermaphroditism, in which she had fully functioning male and female reproductive organs, and she had inseminated herself in order to conceive the four children, whom she thinks of as pure and innocent babies because they are the result of immaculate conception. The psychic abilities of the children are caused by genetic mutations, shifts, and flaws owing to inbreeding. The situation is compounded by the fact that the children's grandfather (who is also their great uncle) was a heavy drug user who may have done genetic damage to himself in that way too, and passed it on to the children through his daughter, their mother. Bobby and Julie find that Frank is also at Dr. Fogarty's, where he has sought refuge.

Complications now intensify as Candy, sensing that he is nearer to Frank, kills everyone in his way: two employees of Dakota & Dakota along with one of their wives, Julie's brother Thomas, and Thomas's roommate. With the help of his sister, Candy finds Frank, Julie, and Bobby at Dr. Fogarty's and kidnaps Julie with the threat that he will kill her unless Frank surrenders to him. He takes Julie to the family home where he holds her, waiting for Frank.

Bobby works out a plan to save Julie (neatly patterning her saving of him in the book's opening), and in the climax he and Frank return to Frank's home. Frank realizes that his mother's presence is still in the home and asks where she is. It turns out that the twin sisters have, along with their pack of symbiotic cats, eaten the mother's corpse so as to make her forever a part of them. Candy, in a rage, kills both of the girls. At this point Frank takes Candy by surprise by reaching out to him and holding his hand. Before Candy can react, Frank teleports with him, composing and decomposing their atoms with such rapidity that they become inextricably mixed. When Frank degenerates, so does Candy. Thus, Julie is rescued because Frank has sacrificed himself for her.

Finally, in the denouement, the reader learns that the police assume that Candy has killed his brother and sister and is on the run, and Bobby and Julie are thus free to carry on with their lives. They sell Dakota & Dakota, and with the money from that plus money that they found in the Pollard house, they buy a beach house on the California coast. At the novel's end Julie has just learned that she is pregnant, and she and Bobby are at peace.

CHARACTER DEVELOPMENT

As a general rule, Dean Koontz's characters tend to be flat (one-dimensional) and static (nonchanging), since his plots are usually incident-driven rather than character-driven. However, a study of his work over time shows a clear move toward greater complexity in characterization. Thomas, Julie's brother with Down's syndrome, is an excellent example of this shift. The prototype for Thomas is Buddy Pellineri of *Night Chills*, a character who, like Thomas, is retarded. However, Buddy is basically a plot convenience. Since he cannot be fully brought under control by subliminal suggestion, because he lacks the verbal skills necessary to comprehend the messages, he is free to report to the heroes the dumping of chemicals in the town reservoir. This is his only function in the novel, and once he has fulfilled it, he is killed off. He is thus a flat character without even a real name to distinguish him, since "Buddy" is a generic term. He stands in marked contrast to Thomas, who is a well-rounded and very touching character, perceptive and brave beyond his limitations. One of the ways Koontz makes Thomas real for the reader is through the poems Thomas composes. He does not have the intelligence to be able to write more than his name, and so he creates his poems from magazine illustrations, cutting out "whole pictures and parts of pictures, arranging them as if they were words, in a series of images. . . . Some of his 'poems' were only five images long, and some involved hundreds of clippings arranged in orderly stanzas or, more often, in loosely structured lines that resembled free verse" (67).

> His composing process is fascinating: he sits alone in his
> room, thinking about making a picture poem that would have
> the feeling of eating ice cream and strawberries, not the taste

but the good feeling, so some day when you didn't have any
ice cream or strawberries, you could just look at the poem
and get that same good feeling even without eating anything.
Of course, you couldn't use pictures of ice cream or strawberries in the poem, because that wouldn't be a poem, that
would be only *saying* how good ice cream and strawberries
made you feel. A poem didn't just say, it showed you and
made you feel. (250)

Buddy is also entranced with pictures, but he uses them passively, looking at them because he cannot understand the words that accompany
them. Thomas uses these same pictures actively to make statements without words.

Thomas is a static character, but ultimately he is the catalyst for change
in Julie and Bobby, and when he dies there is meaning to his death: he
uses it to send the message that they need not fear death and, by not
fearing it, they need not fear life, either. In this way, he embodies the
theme of the novel.

The novel's other major characters are Julie Dakota, Bobby Dakota,
Frank Pollard, and Candy Pollard. Julie and Bobby are the novel's protagonists, or heroes. Each is a well-developed character and each is dynamic: their backgrounds are sketched in, there is much information on
their relationship with each other, and their different attitudes toward
the work they do are credible and serve to individualize them. By the
end of the novel, each has learned something significant about himself
or herself. Bobby has come to see that he is not the easy-going, laid-back
person he thought he was, that underneath he is a person who craves
order and cannot tolerate the chaos of disorder. Julie has come to see
that she and Bobby are complex people, driven by greed as much as by
good intentions, and that in this they are only human. She has also come
to learn that to live for her dream of the future is to overlook the dreams
that have come true for her in the present. At the end of the novel she
is more like the old Bobby in her outlook on life, and he is more like the
old Julie. In this way, they are good examples of characters influencing
one another in realistic ways. They have been married for seven years,
and in seven years we might well expect that partners would undergo
changes as a result of sharing one another's lives.

Frank Pollard, the character who opens the novel and tantalizes the
reader with his amnesia, is too passive to be either a protagonist or an
antagonist; instead, he is best seen as the novel's victim. He is another

well-rounded character, and despite the fact that he has paranormal abilities, he is a realistic character. Koontz draws a believable picture of Frank as the outsider, the only normal-seeming person in his family, but someone who, with respect to the rest of the world, will always be different and "other." He is a lonely person who has spent the last seven years of his life on the run from his brother Candy, a situation that totally dominates his thoughts and actions. When, in the climax, he sacrifices himself to save Julie, his character remains static: the sacrifice is his ultimate escape from Candy, who dies along with Frank.

The antagonist or villain is, of course, Candy, a character who is both flat and static. We know why Candy has a blood lust, but this is all we know about him—everything else about Candy is secondary to this, his defining characteristic. And he remains the same throughout the novel, beginning and ending the story devoted to the memory of his mother and convinced that in his murders of innocent people he is carrying out God's will.

Finally, *The Bad Place* has a number of characters who have small roles but who are fleshed out by being given some unique characteristic that intrigues the reader and gives dimension. The hypnotist Jackie Jaxx, who appears in only one scene of the novel, is a good example of such a person. He sees himself as carrying on the tradition of the great magicians and hypnotists. Even as a child his dream of success was to make it in Las Vegas as a big-time mentalist, something he has succeeded in doing. When he hypnotizes Frank and regresses him in the Dakota & Dakota offices, so that Julie and Bobby might learn who Frank is and what he is running from, the then-terrified Frank teleports. The equally terrified Jackie keeps assuring everyone that Jaxx really does not have the ability to make people disappear, while Jaxx agonizes over whether he can be sued for what has happened. The threat of malpractice suits hangs over everyone these days and such a small detail as this makes Jackie believable and endearing to the reader.

SETTING

Of the Dean Koontz novels examined in this Critical Companion, *The Bad Place* is the richest in setting, both in the way it is used and in the variety of settings included. Nature is used in traditional ways, with an incoming storm prefacing Frank's telling of his story to Julie and Bobby. There's an increase in the intensity of the storm as the strangeness of the story builds. Unusual winds signal that teleportation is about to take place. A violent thunder and lightning storm signals the climax. However, the setting is also used in nontraditonal ways, with abrupt shifts in climate and surroundings emphasizing the abruptness of Frank's teleportations.

One of the most intriguing natural settings is the description of the alien planet on which Bobby and Frank land in Frank's journeyings. Bobby finds himself in a place of fine gray sand covered with red diamonds, and he realizes that it is a quarry. He is surrounded by beetlelike insects as big as a person's hand—creatures programmed for mining the diamonds. The air around him is thick and sulfurous, difficult to breathe. The moon hanging in the sky is "a mottled gray-yellow sphere six times normal size, looming ominously over the land" (282). This description emphasizes the strangeness and other-worldliness of Frank's teleporting abilities, and it highlights the fear and wonder that they induce in Bobby.

Another very effective use of natural setting is the world of animals. Frank and Candy's identical twin sisters, Violet and Verbena, are always seen with their swarm of twenty-six cats, whose mental sensations they share and whose actions they can direct. Through these animals Koontz makes it believable that the sisters live in a world composed almost entirely of sensation—of sleep, grooming, hunting, and feeding. This world is made particularly vivid by the fact that until the age of six, Violet was autistic, so overwhelmed by the rush of sensation from the world around her that she could not sort out the messages coming to her. Her sister Verbena never learns to perform such sorting, and remains autistic for all her life. This identification with cats and wild creatures emphasizes how incredibly "other" the Pollard sisters are; they are as genetically maimed as their brothers, although all of the Pollard children are maimed in different ways.

An especially vivid use of setting combines both the natural and the unnatural worlds. Bobby takes one of the mining beetles from the alien planet to an entomologist, the den of whose home is filled with trays of pinned specimens of various bugs and insects, characterized by Bobby as "many-legged, carapaced, antenna-bristled, mandibled, and thoroughly repulsive" (240). Bobby imagines the dead bugs moving in their glass-covered cases, trying to get at him. From all the shallow drawers in the entomologist's study he hears things moving about, and even though he knows it's only his imagination, "the whispery sounds from the specimen drawers . . . grew louder and more frenzied by the minute"

(247). These sounds are reminiscent of the use of insects in Koontz's novel *Whispers*, with the difference that here they are clearly imaginary and in *Whispers* they are meant to be real.

Both novels make good use of insects, but it is the imaginary insects that are the most convincing. There's no good reason for the mother in *Whispers* to have left all the cockroaches in the root cellar—who wants a cellar full of cockroaches?—except pure sadism toward her children. She could just as effectively control the children by shutting them in an insect-free cellar, since isolation and darkness are terrifying to any child; the only function of the insects is to emphasize the horror of what was done to the children. The insects really are horrifying, though, and when Koontz uses the same image of whispering insects on the verge of swarming over a person in *The Bad Place*, it is very effective: both humorous because it isn't real—it's just in Bobby's imagination—and scary because the thought of swarming insects is creepy and disgusting in and of itself. This mix of humor and terror is far more effective than terror alone, since the mind can take only so much fear and then, out of self-protection, shuts down its responses. But when fear alternates with humor, readers are pulled down into horror and then released, pulled down and then released again. They never feel in control of their own reactions. In making use of these similar insect images in his two novels, Koontz demonstrates his growth as a writer: the second time around the image is both more realistic and more frightening.

The use of artificial setting in the form of people's homes and apartments is particularly varied and effective in *The Bad Place*. The home Julie and Bobby live in is basically a place for transients, a tract house in Orange, California, that they bought for its investment potential. They have furnished only what had to be furnished in order for them to temporarily live in the house. Other than the kitchen, family room, and bedroom, the house stands empty. This setting will, at the end of the novel, help underline the theme that Julie and Bobby have overlooked what life has to offer them in the present in pursuit of their fantasies of future offerings.

Another example of a home that shelters no one is the abandoned apartment house, waiting to be demolished, that Frank hides out in at the beginning of the novel. And the strange Pollard children live in an equally strange house. Isolated, decrepit, and decaying, it could be straight out of *Psycho*; along with death, it is the bad place of the title. The only person who lives in a normal home is Dr. Fogarty, and his quaint, homey place is used to contrast with the doctor himself, who turns out to be another of the many psychopaths who make up the Koontz world. The discrepancy between the doctor's home and his character creates a sense that nothing may be what it seems to be in this novel.

POINT OF VIEW

Koontz often uses the third-person omniscient point of view, but in *The Bad Place* he alternates the characters on whom his unknown narrator focuses to tell the story: Chapter 1 focuses on Frank Pollard, Chapter 2 on Bobby Dakota, Chapter 3 on Frank again, Chapter 4 on Bobby, and Chapter 5 returns to Pollard. Chapter 6 then switches the focus to Julie, Chapter 7 goes back to Frank, and Chapter 8 again returns to Bobby. The story line continues to alternate between these three characters until Chapter 13, which focuses on Candy, so that there are now four characters who alternate as the center of the narrative—Frank, Bobby, Julie, and Candy.

In Chapter 22 the focus shifts again, this time to Julie's brother Thomas, and here Koontz switches to a new point of view, third-person limited, in which Thomas tells the story and the reader sees everything through the mind of Thomas. Koontz then returns to the use of third-person omniscient, adding yet a new character as focal point in Chapter 26—Candy and Frank's sister Violet—and the novel now alternates between six characters—Frank, Bobby, Julie, Candy, Thomas, and Violet—until Chapter 29, which centers on Dakota & Dakota operative Clint Karaghiosis and his colleague, Hal Yamataka. Chapter 42 adds another operative, computer expert Lee Chen. In Chapter 49 the focus shifts yet again, this time to Felina Karaghiosis, the wife of Clint, and the final chapter concentrates on Julie and Bobby. Overall, then, two different kinds of third-person point of view are used in this novel—third-person limited and third-person omniscient—and the story focuses on the subplots of ten separate characters.

This shifting of point of view and focus may seem confusing, but in practice it is an effective technique for allowing the reader to experience what Candy experiences when he kills; to enter the strange, sensation-based, shared mind of his identical twin sisters; and to be filled with awe at the rich inner world of Thomas, a world we would otherwise have no access to since Thomas lacks the language ability to describe it to the reader in words. The switch to third-person limited is also effective in its suggestion that Thomas's world is so special only Thomas is capable of showing it to us. Seeing the novel from so many different angles creates a rich, multilayered narrative voice that in its complexity mirrors the complexity of the novel's three subplots. It is an effective tool for illustrating one of the novel's underlying messages: the real world is one of chaos, but nonetheless we manage to create order out of it and make sense of it.

THEMATIC ISSUES

The theme of *The Bad Place* is explicitly stated, not once but a number of times, and it is both simple and profound: to live for tomorrow is to miss out on living for today. It is a rejection of life by those who are so afraid of dying that they deny themselves any real living, but to live life fully requires acceptance of the inevitability of death. At the end of the novel Thomas, on the verge of dying, has a near-death experience in which he sees that death is not after all the Bad Place, that it is light and warmth and love. This is the message that he sends to Julie through Bobby, and it is this that enables them to live in the chaos of life.

ALTERNATIVE READING: ALLEGORY

Given that it is far more usual to imply theme than to state it, one question raised by *The Bad Place* is why Koontz has broken with this pattern. What does the novel gain by such a direct statement? One answer to this question is that the novel is more than the story of Frank Pollard and what is frightening him. It is also an allegory, and it is conventional in literature to state the meaning of an allegory explicitly.

An allegory is a story that works on more than one level. In addition to the literal meaning of the story itself, it has a second meaning in which characters, events, and setting represent ideas and concepts beyond themselves. The most famous allegory in English literature is Bunyon's *Pilgrim's Progress* (1678). In this story the protagonist, Christian, achieves salvation by fleeing the City of Destruction and journeying with much travail to the Celestial City. On his journey he must pass through such places as the Slough of Despond, the Valley of Humiliation, the Valley of the Shadow of Death, Vanity Fair, and the Doubting Castle. He meets many people on the way, among them Mr. Wordly Wiseman, Faithful,

Hopeful, Giant Despair, and Greatheart. J. A. Cuddon sums up *Pilgrim's Progress* when he says, "The whole work is a simplified representation . . . of the average man's journey through the trials and tribulations of life on his way to heaven" (1991, 23). As with all true allegory, the tale is effective as a tale—that is, as a record of what happens to Christian. It is also effective as a story that teaches every human being how to achieve salvation. Cuddon further notes of allegory as a literary form that its origins are very ancient and that "it appears to be a mode of expression (a way of feeling and thinking about things and seeing them) so natural to the human mind that it is universal" (1991, 23).

In addition to religious allegories such as *Pilgrim's Progress* there are political allegories, in which each character represents a political figure, movement, or concern. (George Orwell's *Animal Farm* is a classic example of this type of allegory.) In moral allegories each character represents a particular moral virtue; one could create a moral allegory about professional sports, in which one character represents greed, another unbridled competition, and a third, sportmanship and fair play. Satirical allegories set up stories that make a sharp critical point about society, such as Robert Coover's *The Universal Baseball Association, Inc., J. Henry Waugh, Prop.* (1968), in which baseball is used to satirize attitudes toward religion in America. It is possible to construct an allegory about virtually anything, so long as there are two levels of story—one the literal, event-by-event narrative and one the concepts or ideas that the events represent.

In Dean Koontz's *The Bad Place* the literal story is the narrative of Frank Pollard waking up in an alley, hiring Dakota & Dakota to help him find out who he is, and so on. There are also a number of elements in the story that are not essential to this first level, but that are essential to a second level of meaning, the allegorical level. Among these elements is the persistent reference to The Dream, a term that changes meaning throughout the book and is only defined in the denouement. Initially, The Dream is envisioned as money: Julie and Bobby spend no money on their home or themselves so that they can reinvest everything in Dakota & Dakota, not because that is an end in itself but, rather, because it will enable them to build it into a major firm that can be sold at a large profit. Next The Dream is defined as a place: they will use the money to buy a simple house by the sea. And, The Dream is defined as people: Julie and Bobby will live in the house with Thomas, Julie's institutionalized brother. Besides this, Julie and Bobby also conceive of The Dream as their recognition of the inevitability of death and the uncertainty of what may or may not follow. Given that there is no guarantee of any life beyond this one—that death may be the ultimate end—The Dream represents paradise for the Dakotas, since they believe that such an earthly paradise is the only one that humans can be certain of.

In addition to these meanings, there is a literal dream, a nightmare, that takes place in Chapter 23 and is also introduced as The Dream. In this version, The Dream foreshadows the coming of Candy and actual death for Julie and Bobby. In this guise it represents not only the inevitability of death for all creatures but also the specific deaths of the Dakotas. Then, in Chapter 51, The Dream comes to stand for compulsion when Julie recognizes that she and Bobby are pursuing the Pollard case not out of concern for Frank but because it is "a once-in-a-lifetime shot at really big bucks, the Main Chance for which every hustler in the world was looking and which most of them would never find" (334). Thus, The Dream also represents moral ambiguity, and Julie wonders if achieving The Dream in this way might not spoil it, have it be less than it might have been. Nevertheless, she cannot turn away from the case because she will not relinquish The Dream. For Bobby, The Dream has yet another meaning, that of order and peace, to be achieved by leaving the chaos of everyday life. In this context, The Dream represents illusion, since it is set in juxtaposition to the real world.

Characters other than Julie and Bobby have dreams in the novel as well. Clint Karaghiosis, an operative for Dakota & Dakota, says of California, "Everyone's got a dream, and the one more people have than any other is the California dream, so they never stop coming, even though so many have come now that the dream isn't really quite attainable any more" (230). So here, too, a dream represents both place and illusion—the state of California and a life there that is no longer attainable. Clint also has a dream: his wife is deaf, and he dreams that one day there will be advances in medical science that will enable her to hear. Since he and his wife are both killed by Candy, this dream proves to be an illusion.

Two other elements to the allegory that turn out to be closely connected are the Bad Thing and the Bad Place. In Bobby's nightmare about Julie dying, a voice keeps shouting to him, "BADTHINGBADTHINGBADTHINGBADTHING!" (100). It is the voice of Thomas, warning Bobby so that he can protect Julie. Thomas can telepathically reach out to Candy Pollard's mind and see that he intends harm for Julie. For Thomas, Candy is conceptualized as the Bad Thing, "A man but not a man. Something very bad. Ugly-nasty." Thomas fears that Candy will take Julie to the Bad Place and he specifically says that the Bad Place is death: "Hell was *a* bad place, but Death was *the* Bad Place." He goes on to imagine it as being like the night, "all that big empty" (140–41). Here, Thomas is reiterating Julie and Bobby's belief that after death there is nothing. Frank also identifies Candy with death, saying, "He's death walking, he's death living" (260), and of the house where Frank grew up and Candy still lives Frank says, "Look at it, my God, what a place, what a dark place, what a bad place" (259). Thus, the Bad Thing is Candy, an agent of death who will take Julie to the Bad Place, to her death, to the big empty.

The allegory now consists of The Dream, a concept of Eden as a specific earthly place wherein Bobby and Julie can escape the chaos of life and the certainty of nothingness after death. It also consists of the Bad Thing, a death bringer who assures escape from chaos, since death is conceived as a nothingness and not even chaos can exist in nothingness. And the allegory consists of the Bad Place, the place of death. This is a desperately bleak picture of human life and its possibilities for happiness. In this model, the best that Julie and Bobby can hope for is to escape into illusion, into the world of The Dream. But there is one more element to this allegory, the character of Thomas. It is through Thomas that the reader sees both the Bad Thing and the Bad Place and, finally, it is because Thomas has the courage to confront both of these entities that the true nature of the Bad Place can be seen. At the moment of dying, Thomas calls out to Bobby and through him to Julie that death is not the great empty—that instead it is a place of light and of love. Thomas's final message to his beloved sister is that only by accepting death can one embrace life. In this sense, Thomas's role in the allegory is to be The Messenger who brings the Word, explaining that there is a life hereafter and, therefore, we can bear to live in this world and be happy here. We are not doomed to live here in terror and dread, hiding from our inevitable fates. Julie and Bobby receive and accept the message, living in their house by the sea with both chaos and order, and "dreaming the biggest dream of all—that people never really die" (417). Finally, then, The Dream is immortality, and in this allegorical reading, The Messenger meets with the Bad Thing in the Bad Place and sends back the message that The Dream is not an illusion after all. It exists and it is available to all of us. In this sense, The Messenger is also a Christ figure, bringing to human beings the promise of life everlasting.

Mr. Murder
(1993)

Of the sixty novels Dean Koontz has written, under his own name and under ten pseudonyms (see Bibliography), his two favorite works are *Watchers* (1987) and *Mr. Murder* (1993). He says of them,

> Writing a novel is usually an emotional roller coaster. Some days you think it's fine, some days you think it's mediocre, and some days you think it stinks; you soar with exhilaration and quickly plunge into despair. But with both [*Watchers* and *Mr. Murder*], the story came like a great wide river, flowing smooth and swift, and for the whole ride I knew I was going somewhere special. There are other books of my own that I like as well or nearly as well as those two, but *Watchers* and *Mr. Murder* were composed with so much *confidence* compared to other books that I'll always love them a little more and be unable to rank them objectively. (Gorman interview, 47).

In fact, the two books have a good deal in common. Both are centered on biologically engineered characters who have been developed by human beings for the use of human beings, and who suffer loneliness, pain, and a terrible sense of being nothing, of belonging to no species. Both works are also very much interested in the concept of doubling and both pose this concept in Christian terms of good and evil, of the split between soul and body, where the human soul is seen as a symbol of purity, the human body as a symbol of corruption.

In *Watchers* the doubles are Einstein, the dog, and The Outsider. Each has been genetically engineered to be used as a weapon, but the dog has the advantage of looking like a dog, looking normal, and so he can conceal his otherness. A noble character, he is a symbol of goodness. The Outsider is grotesque in appearance, and knows that it is. It can pass as nothing other than a monster, and it is desperately envious of the dog, who has choices not available to it. In its viciousness The Outsider is the symbol of evil, and in its pain it is the symbol of the evil of human beings, who would create a creature such as this. This pair, the dog and The Outsider, are similar to the central characters of *Mr. Murder*, Marty Stillwater and Alfie.

Marty is a mystery writer who lives in California, and Alfie is an operable clone (hence his name—he is the *alpha*, or first of these) who has been genetically developed from Marty's blood and bone marrow cells. His function is to be an assassin, controlled by his creators, who have programmed him to exist entirely under their direction. He is physically identical to Marty, and like The Outsider, he knows that he is somehow other—that although he looks human, he is not human. He wants desperately to have a real life and be a real person, and he is, perhaps through telepathy, aware of the existence of Marty, his double. He decides that Marty has stolen his life, his wife, his children, and his profession, and that he must kill Marty to gain them back. In this pairing, it is Marty who is the symbol of good and Alfie who is the symbol of evil. This again follows the pattern of Christian symbolism, since Alfie exists only as a physical being; he lacks a soul. And like The Outsider, Alfie symbolizes not only evil in himself but also evil in human beings, since it is they who have created him.

Yet another example of doubling in *Mr. Murder* is the Christmas story that Marty is writing for his children, "Santa's Evil Twin," in which Santa's physically identical twin is making of Christmas a time of misery and pain rather than joy and celebration. Here, too, the pairing is specifically identified in terms of good and evil. And finally, when Marty is interviewed by *People* magazine (which creates the title of Mr. Murder for him, reflecting the fact that he writes mysteries), the article includes a photo of him that is out of focus and deliberately makes him look grotesque and monstrous. Thus, he too is, at least in this context, considered to be an outsider and something other than human, on the basis of his stories. There is some suggestion then that to create monsters is to be a monster, although with Marty this is only implied, showing that there is a difference between the creations of fiction and reality. This message is also one of the messages of *Watchers*; indeed, in both books Dean Koontz is saying to the reader, "Be very careful to keep your fantasies securely within the world of fantasy."

Koontz's fascination with doubling can also be seen in his novel *Whispers* (1980), in which the antagonist, Bruno Frye, turns out to be an identical twin. He and his twin have been raised to believe that they are one person. The result of such psychological manipulation and distortion of self is that the two become psychopathic killers who, through their murders, attempt to destroy the person who so shaped (or misshaped) them. Like The Outsider and Alfie, the dual Bruno character is also aware of its otherness and is both a source of evil and a victim of evil. Koontz draws him compassionately, showing the horror of what has been done to him. This early example of the double does not, however, have the good-evil combination that appears in the two later novels, suggesting that in these two works Koontz has followed a pattern that he has followed before, wherein he takes a particular concept, works it out in a particular way, and then returns to it later to explore another aspect of it. (A comparable example of Koontz's returning to a topic and reconsidering it occurs in the novels *Phantoms* and *Hideaway*, and is discussed in Chapter 3.)

GENRE

Like nearly all of Dean Koontz's later novels, *Mr. Murder* is a cross-genre novel (see Chapter 2) that fits best in the suspense category, a broad group covering works that include elements of many different genres. It is a mystery in that a central element of the novel is the question of what it is that is pulling Alfie to California, and of how a cryptic message to Marty that first warns him of something being wrong appears on his tape recorder. It is a police procedural, in that it is realistic in its description of how the police react when Marty tells them about his double, and of why the police are unlikely to believe him, as well as in its description of some of the litigation the contemporary police are likely to face in the ordinary performance of their duties. It is a technothriller in its careful, accurate descriptions of the use of the tools of high technology for the locating and tracking of Alfie. It falls into the hard-science subgenre of science fiction, since it looks at what might be done by an extension of genetic engineering, a field of contemporary biology. It falls into another science fiction subgenre, that of the dystopia or negative society, in its use of psychology to manipulate human beings rather than to benefit them, its use of science to create human monsters, and its bleak conclusion that suggests little hope for society as a whole. Certainly the novel also fits the soft-science subgenre of science fiction that concerns itself with extrasensory perception, since Alfie is in contact with Marty through ESP. And finally, *Mr. Murder* is a novel of political intrigue and terrorism in its concern with how various political factions might respond to current political problems.

PLOT DEVELOPMENT

Mr. Murder opens with the original situation (the world of the work of fiction before something happens to disrupt it) of the hero or protagonist, Marty Stillwater. He is at home in his office, working on what will be his new book, as he does every day. A mystery writer who seems on the verge of making it big, Stillwater's last two paperback novels have made the best-seller list, and everyone expects his new book to be his first hardcover best-seller. On this day his wife has taken the children to the movies, and he is in the process of dictating a letter to his editor.

The initial major complication puts into play a whole series of further complications. In *Mr. Murder* this initial complication occurs when Marty realizes that he has been saying over and over into a tape recorder, "I need, I need," and he has no recollection of having done this, nor does he have any idea of what he was referring to, of what it is he needs. He is afraid that he is suffering from fugue, a psychological state in which a person suffers from blackouts during which he or she acts normally but later has no memory of what was done, who was there, what the circumstances were. Marty's fear leads him to behave uncharacteristically, snapping at his wife and children. Now Marty begins to have psychic attacks, in which he is slammed by a wall of terror. He goes to his doctor, afraid that he may be suffering from a brain tumor, but everything seems to be normal.

While these odd fugue states and terror attacks are occurring to Marty, a killer is in the Midwest going about his usual routine of assassinating victims who have been chosen for him, although he does not know who chooses them or why they must die, nor does he know who he himself is, or how he came to be an assassin. He completes his task in Kansas

City, but then he behaves uncharacteristically and, instead of following routine, gets in his car and starts driving west. He has a compulsion to do this, although again, he does not know why.

The killer turns out to be Alfie, a genetically engineered murderer who was cloned from Marty's blood and bone marrow cells. (Marty had been in the same hospital where the cells that were supposed to be used for the engineering of the killer were extracted. By mistake, his cell samples had been switched with those intended for Alfie.) Alfie is an exact replica of Marty, and somehow he is in psychic communication with him and knows of his existence in California. While Alfie doesn't understand why he feels compelled to go to where Marty is, he does know that something is wrong with him, that he is incomplete and lacks a real life. His efforts to create a real life for himself cause greater and greater complications. First, Alfie reaches the Stillwater home and breaks in, familiarizing himself with the life that he is convinced has been stolen from him. He finds pictures of Marty's wife and children and copies of his books, complete with pictures of the author on the back covers that look exactly like Alfie. But when he sits at Marty's desk, he cannot write as Marty does; the words will not come.

At this point, Marty returns from his doctor's appointment and walks in on Alfie. Alfie looks at him and says, "What now? Do we somehow become one person, fade into each other, like in some crazy science-fiction movie . . . or do I just kill you and take your place? . . . And if I kill you . . . do the memories you've stolen from me become mine again, when you're dead? If I kill you . . . am I made whole?" (124–25). Alfie moves from questioning to aggression, and Marty shoots him, hitting him in the chest, but Alfie doesn't even fall, although he is covered in blood. A struggle ensues and Alfie goes over a balcony railing, landing flat on his back and fracturing his spine. He has also lost a great deal of blood from the gunshot wounds. Marty leaves to call the police, and when he returns, Alfie has disappeared. When the police arrive, it becomes obvious that they think Marty has invented a story in order to create publicity for himself, that there is no factual basis for what he reports. This terrifies Marty, since he knows Alfie is real and will be back. When the police leave, Marty and his wife begin to pack up, convinced that they must get away at once before Alfie returns. They are correct in their assumption; as they are packing, Alfie comes and abducts their two daughters. Marty succeeds in rescuing the girls, and the family abandons their home, trying to get very far from Alfie. They head for Mammoth Lakes, a small rural town where Marty's parents live.

Meanwhile, Alfie's handlers—members of a clandestine right-wing political group known as the Network—realize that he is no longer following the standard operating procedures he has been programmed for. What is worse, he has disappeared. They begin to track him, determined to reprogram him and, if that fails, destroy him. While they are doing this they see an article on Marty in *People* magazine and realize that there is some connection between Alfie and Marty, although they do not know what it is. Nonetheless, they research Marty's background in the hope of finding Alfie, and decide that Marty would probably go to his parents in Mammoth Lakes if he were seeking a sanctuary. Alfie, still in telepathic contact with Marty, follows him and the stage is set for all the players to come together.

In Mammoth Lakes, the Network, the first of the players to arrive, has set up a surveillance vehicle outside Marty's parents's home. When Alfie arrives he recognizes it at once for what it is and kills the operatives inside. Then he enters the house. When Marty's parents see that something is wrong, that he is a very different Marty from the person they raised, Alfie kills them. He is convinced that the "other" Marty, who in his mind is the fake Marty, has somehow gotten to them before he did and poisoned their minds. He follows the trail of Marty and his family, who have gone to ground in a cabin in the nearby mountains. Alfie's primary handlers reach Mammoth Lakes, find their dead operatives, and track Alfie to an abandoned religious commune, where he has cornered the Stillwaters at the top of a bell tower.

In the climax, Alfie is killed by his two handlers just before he can kill Marty. They begin to put into place the planned execution of the Stillwaters, so that the case will be closed and the police will ask no awkward questions that might lead to exposure of the Network. At this moment, one of the handlers, Clocker, turns on the other and kills him, in this way saving the Stillwater family.

Finally, in the denouement, the surviving operative Clocker helps the Stillwaters escape to a safe place, later providing them with false identities. He tells them that they can never return to their old lives, since even though Alfie has been destroyed and he was the only operative clone the Network had developed, there may be unknown members of the Network who are harboring grudges, determined to avenge themselves on the Stillwaters when it becomes safe to do so. Under their new names, Marty becomes the author of successful children's books illustrated by his wife. Clocker disappears, leaving as enigmatically as he came, and subsequently a book of fiction is published that seems to be a sort of *Star Trek* approach to the topic of cloning. Through documents that Clocker has stolen, and presumably, Marty has organized and summarized, the Network is publicly exposed and, at least for the moment, its power is destroyed. The mysterious disappearance of the author Martin Stillwater becomes yet another popular legend returned to year after year but never producing final answers, much like the disappearance of union figure Jimmy Hoffa. All that the public knows about Marty is that once there was such a person, and now that person is no more.

One specific issue raised by *Mr. Murder* is its ending. Usually, Dean Koontz ends his novels with a resolution that is, in one way or another, brought about by the action of the protagonists. Through their bravery and persistence, they succeed in containing evil; they are the central characters of the story, and they bring about its closure. This is not the case in *Mr. Murder*, though. Here, Koontz uses what is known as a *deus ex machina* ending. This is a term taken from the ancient Greek theater, where gods who intervened in the actions of humans, rescuing them from what seemed to be hopeless situations, were lowered by a structure (or "machine") to the stage below. *Deus ex machina* is a Latin phrase meaning "god from the machine." In literary analysis it is used to describe a sudden ending that the reader has not been prepared for and that resolves a problem that seemed headed for deadlock. It is in this sense a magical ending: someone steps in, just like a magician, and makes things all better; the magician waves a wand, and the lady in the box who was just sawed in half is shown to be whole after all.

In *Mr. Murder*, Karl Clocker is the god or magician who steps in. The Stillwaters are in a bell tower with Alfie. They have done everything that they can to save themselves and now Alfie is about to triumph; in fact, he is on the verge of cannibalizing Marty when Oslett and Clocker suddenly appear. Oslett kills Alfie, and then turns his gun on the Stillwaters, ready now to kill them too, when out of the blue Clocker shoots Oslett. The reader has been given no indication up to this point that Clocker is anything but a loyal operative of the Network, and the ending is jarring in its convenience. It feels as though Koontz had to get the Stillwaters out of their predicament in some way, and so he turned to Clocker because he could think of nothing else. However, anyone who, like Dean Koontz, has written over fifty novels, clearly has had a good deal of experience creating endings, and it is therefore unlikely that he chose this ending for lack of another alternative. Perhaps instead his intention is to show how very dangerous the Network is—so dangerous that escaping from it is dependent on luck and the grace of God as well as one's own efforts. While it may be true that God helps those who help themselves, faced with any force as powerful and all-encompassing as the Network, salvation requires both parts of the equation—that is, the help of God (or the magical intervention of fate) and oneself.

CHARACTER DEVELOPMENT

Dean Koontz's later works, such as *Mr. Murder* (1993) and *Dark Rivers of the Heart* (1994), mark a continued growth in his concern with character development. The protagonists of *Mr. Murder* are Marty Stillwater, his wife Paige, and Karl Clocker, who begins life as an antagonist but changes roles at the end of the novel. Marty is a mystery writer who is basically a simple person: he loves his wife and family, he is a very good father and husband, he has a profession that he is both happy with and successful at, and he is on the verge of going from being successful to being very, very successful—a famous writer who will be known by people who don't even read his books. He is a well-rounded character despite his lack of complexity, and is almost the epitome of a normal person: happy, well-adjusted, looking forward to tomorrow. He is the last person one would expect to find caught up in an espionage plot; the unusual things in his world take place in the fiction he creates, not in his own life.

Marty is a dynamic character to the extent that, when he is confronted with Alfie and the possibility that his life will be destroyed, he finds within himself the strength to fight back to save what is his. This is not a change, though, but a predictable development of the person he is. He is described as a man for whom family and a settled home life are paramount, and so it is no surprise when he risks everything to protect this. When he and his wife go into sanctuary and take on new identities, he remains essentially the person he was. He is still a writer, but now he concentrates solely on children's stories and no longer writes mysteries. Although circumstances force him to be a loner, this is no big transition, since he is a person who has always disliked publicity and who was embarrassed by the attention he received in magazines such as *People*. The insight he has gained that justifies defining him as a dynamic character is the knowledge he now has about the world of politics and government. He understands that both can be all-powerful and at the same time so secretive that they can be seen only by the effects they cause;

exactly who has caused a given effect is likely to be a matter of conjecture and almost never a matter of certainty.

His wife, Paige Stillwater, is also a round, dynamic character. Dean Koontz often has strong women characters in his novels, and Paige is a good example. Where Marty has had a happy, secure childhood, Paige's has been unhappy and dysfunctional. Her parents were cold, distant, and abusive, and when she was sixteen, her father killed her mother and then committed suicide. Paige was the one who found them when she came home from school. An aunt she did not like was named as her guardian, and Paige then went to court to be declared an adult so that she could be her own guardian.

The Network operative who is the source of this information (they are discussing her to see how much of a problem she may be to them in their effort to eliminate first Alfie, then the Stillwaters) says, "The judge was sufficiently impressed with her to rule in her favor. It's rare but it does happen" (340). And when another operative comments that Paige must have had an excellent lawyer, the first agrees and tells him that Paige was her own lawyer. Clearly, even as an adolescent she was a strong person capable of taking responsibility for the conditions of her life. She is now a child psychologist, and has supported Marty in the early years of his writing, while he established himself. When the family is trying to escape from Alfie, Paige plays as significant a role as Marty, lying in wait for the clone while Marty takes the children to safety, since the clone can sense Marty but cannot sense Paige, and so she will have the element of surprise. And although both her efforts and Marty's are only partly successful in destroying Alfie, they are successful to the same extent: this is clearly an equal partnership.

When the family goes into sanctuary, the changes in Paige's life are greater than those in Marty's. Unlike him, she leaves what was her profession and no longer practices as a psychologist, but has instead become a book illustrator. And where her work in psychology took her out into the world and put her in contact with many different people, she now lives a far more reclusive life. She has also learned that her self-sufficiency has limits. Even though she could as a girl overcome the power of the judicial system, there is little she can do to overcome the power of the Network, the power of fanatics who do not show themselves. Nonetheless, she has found contentment in the new life that she and Marty have created for themselves and their family.

Karl Clocker is in many ways the most intriguing of the protagonists in *Mr. Murder*. He is a huge, hulking man who has a talent for violence and who, for that reason, "was a man of his times" (177). He is a fine example of Koontz taking what might be a stock character—the shadowy operative whose profession defines him—and adding depth by giving him unanticipated interests and personality characteristics. Clocker is a quiet, self-contained person who seldom talks. On the occasions when he does so, he is so cryptic that little communication takes place. But Koontz has also made him a *Star Trek* fan and on this topic, he can talk forever; he knows the plots of all the movies and television episodes, and spends his time while on surveillance reading *Star Trek* novels. He is paired with another network operative who loathes anything to do with *Star Trek*, and this becomes the basis for some fine humor in what is really a grim book. And since readers are familiar with the *Star Trek* series, Clocker's cryptic comments are not nearly as inscrutable to the reader as they are to his Network colleague. We understand that Clocker is making fun of the intensely serious colleague, a preppy Princeton graduate who is uncomfortable with the world of fiction and fantasy. When the graduate asks Clocker when they'll be arriving somewhere, he says, "Half an hour, forty minutes—assuming the fabric of reality doesn't warp between here and there" (265).

Very little substantive information is provided on Clocker. He says that he has always wanted a life of adventure, and that is why he joined the Network. He says that all along he has intended to expose the Network, but he does not say why he wanted this life, where he received his training for it, or what his life was like before this. Nonetheless, the information given about Clocker is so entertaining that we feel we know him—how could we not know someone we like so well? He is thus a good example of a minor character who feels well developed because he has a quality—in this case, his *Trek*kerdom—that readers can relate to immediately. He is also an example of a static character, since he has planned all along to betray the Network and this is exactly what he does at the end. (Of course, he would seem dynamic to his Network colleagues, who have no idea of his real intentions.)

Mr. Murder has three other antagonists: Clocker's colleague Drew Oslett, police lieutenant Cyrus Lowbock, and the major villain, Alfie. A well-developed and round character, in many ways Alfie is a child. He is a genetically engineered assassin who has been in the field only fourteen months. He has no sense of who he is, only of what he does: he kills people on command. Despite his acts Alfie is a pitiful character because he knows that there is something wrong with him, that something is lacking. He goes to movies to try to learn what it is like to be human, but he receives mixed messages. Should he be the gentle Jimmy Stewart or the violent Sylvester Stallone? He is lonely and tortured, and he doesn't even know his name. As it turns out, he has been given no real name. He is just Alfie, the alpha or first of what is intended to be a series of human clones developed for specific purposes.

Although Alfie has been designed to have extraordinary recuperative powers and can be killed only by a direct hit to his brain, he is a classic example of technology gone wrong, since his handlers no longer have control of him. In being unable to totally eradicate his human emotions and needs, they have created a monster who potentially threatens everyone. Clocker says of Alfie, "The first operative Alpha-generation human clone is a renegade, mutating in ways we might not understand, and capable of infecting the human gene pool with genetic material that could spawn a new and thoroughly hostile race of nearly invulnerable super beings" (362), and no one disagrees with him. Although Alfie escapes the control of his handlers, he is a static character, since he escapes at the opening of the story and therefore the only Alfie the reader knows is the renegade Alfie. He begins the story determined to create a human life for himself, and he ends it with this determination. His plea is the same at the beginning of the book as it is at the end: "I need, I need, I need."

A second villain is the Network operative Drew Oslett. As with Clocker, very little information is given about him and he plays a small role in the story, so he might well have been a stock character—a shadowy high-tech operative working for an equally shadowy, high-tech organization. But the individual quirks that Koontz gives him make him seem like a real person, someone the reader might well know. These quirks are his love of fast, glitzy, high-tech equipment, games, and lifestyles. A graduate of Princeton and Harvard, he thinks very well of himself and is sure that it is through some error, some careless oversight, that he has been given a plodding *Trek*ker like Clocker as a partner. (He even considers killing Clocker, but decides he doesn't have the time right now—that finding Alfie takes precedence over getting a more appropriate partner.) Just as Alfie seeks to create a life for himself through films, Oslett creates his through the constant sensory input of the media. His favorite film is *Lethal Weapon 3*, which he loves because there's no story line to follow, he doesn't have to get involved with the characters, and it is full of violent, extremely loud action sequences. He also delights in equipment, and there's a wonderful scene in which Oslett buys himself ski clothes so as to be prepared for the weather in Mammoth Lakes. He is entranced by the various and sundry high-tech features of the clothing.

It is easy for the reader to identify with such characteristics and for this reason Oslett is far more than the stereotyped operative he might have been. Nonetheless, he is a flat character. Like Alfie and Clocker, he is static, ending the novel as he began it, with no new insights into himself or the way the world works.

An interesting, although again minor, antagonist is someone whom the reader might well have expected to be a protagonist, the plainclothes police detective Cyrus Lowbock. He appears in the novel in only one scene, but his impact is greater than this would indicate, since his cynicsm adds to the story's bleak worldview. It is a staple of the police procedural that individual police are often disillusioned about the criminal justice system, the political power structure, and the likelihood of reforming criminals. But Lowbock takes this disillusionment one step further by being thoroughly cynical about the victims of crime. He is convinced that Marty is inventing the story of Alfie as a way to get publicity, and Lowbock's main concern is not to find the truth but rather to protect himself, to make sure that he is not professionally vulnerable in any way in his handling of the case. He explains to Marty that nowadays police are sued for what they do, for what they do not do, and for anything in between. In Lowbock, Koontz creates a person charged with protecting the public who is interested only in protecting himself and who will take no action rather than have it be the wrong action. This is such a surprising stance for a police officer to take that it catches the reader's attention and makes of Lowbock a rich character, despite the fact that he is basically flat, a character of whom we know very little. He is also a static character, since he appears in only this one scene and any insights he may come to as a result of the case are gained outside of the reader's field of vision.

Finally, the Network itself can be seen as an antagonist. It is, according to Clocker, made up of people who hold power in the establishment—that is, in government, business, and the media, and who are convinced that democracy can no longer work, that the mass of people cannot be trusted to govern themselves, that the world of high technology has made obsolete the world of government by the people. The Network has instituted a number of research programs designed to enable it to quietly take over the positions of power in America, and Alfie was intended as one small part of this, the first of the obedient, engineered police and soldiers who would serve the Network. Of course, the Network is a flat character, since there is no information on how it originated, how these people came into contact with one another, or what has caused them to take the stance they have taken. It is static, since at no point does the Network admit that it might be wrong in its assessments. This use of a group in the traditional role of a character is typical of the way in which organizations take on the role of characters in the world of the technothriller, where their motives and workings intrigue the reader as much as those of a person.

SETTING

Like many of Dean Koontz's novels, *Mr. Murder* is set in California—in this case the peaceful town of Mission Viejo in the southern part of the state. The fact that the killer is stalking the Stillwaters in such a normal, middle-class neighborhood makes his actions all the more frightening. We do not expect violence in an area like this, and the fact that the local police will not help the Stillwaters is terrifying. If good, solid middle-class citizens cannot depend on the police for help, the world is a very dangerous place indeed. When the Stillwaters leave for Mammoth Lakes in California's Sierra Nevadas, they find only a qualified safety. While they do succeed in defeating Alfie, it is at the very high cost of losing Marty's parents, whom Alfie kills. And they cannot remain there, since the Network operatives will be sure to hunt them down. Thus, the peaceful mountain retreat is only a temporary place of safety, and this increases our fear, since it seems that no place is safe for the Stillwaters. When they ultimately find sanctuary, it is as other people, living under other names, in rural Wyoming. So although the countryside is an escape from violence, it is so only as long as no one knows who they are. Ultimately, there is no escape from the Network.

In terms of weather, Koontz has used it in routine ways in *Mr. Murder*. A rain storm when Paige is driving the children home signifies that something bad is happening there, and so it is—Alfie is in the house. And as the story comes closer and closer to its climax, the weather becomes worse and worse, culminating in a heavy snowstorm in the mountains. These events basically serve as window dressing, though. They help set the tone of what is happening in the story, but they do not cause any of the events.

In contrast to his use of weather, Koontz makes imaginative use of clothing and costumes in *Mr. Murder*, especially in his description of Karl Clocker. A large, hulking man, Clocker is given to wearing tweed jackets with leather buttons and leather patches on the elbows, very loud sweater vests with bold diamond-shaped patterns, bright socks that clash with his sweaters, suede Hush Puppies, and hats with little feathers tucked in the brim. His clothing alone drives the dapper Drew Oslett mad, and it raises the question of exactly what sort of person Clocker is—he doesn't sound like the usual hit man and as it will turn out, he is not.

Clothing is also used to establish the character of the self-protective police detective, Cyrus Lowbock. Koontz says that in his gray cords, black loafers, and navy blue cable-stitched sweater he looks like a model for tasteful luxury items such as Rolls-Royces. He adds, "He looked less like any popular image of a cop than like a man who had been born to wealth and knew how to manage and preserve it" (162). While there is no information given on how much money Lowbock has, he certainly does know how to manage and preserve his professional status in the police department and is far more concerned with how he will appear than with whom he can help. Clothing details such as these are an efficient way to give readers a sense of what someone is like, especially when the person is a minor figure.

A final element of setting is the tools, weapons, and equipment that characters use. Again, much can be shown about a person through descriptions of that person's choices. Clocker, for example, uses an atypical gun for a hit man, and of course he will turn out to be an atypical hit man. Oslett's love of sensory input comes through in his surveillance tools. He uses an electronic map to track Alfie, a Satellite Assisted Tracking Unit that isn't available to the general public, and he is delighted with its colorful, well-designed screen; it reminds him of a video game and of the arcades he loves to visit. The suggestion is that he is a grown-up who has not really grown up, that he is a fine example of the yuppy slogan, "He who dies with the most toys wins," and this turns out to be an accurate reading of Oslett's personality. He has no sense of people, only of things. Because of this he loses control of Alfie without realizing it, and also cannot read his partner Karl Clocker, a failure that ultimately leads him to his death.

POINT OF VIEW

Mr. Murder is told from the third-person omniscient point of view. This point of view allows the reader to see into Alfie's mind and understand the pain he feels, something that no other character in the story could show us. It also makes clear the hold movies have on him, and the misleading models they provide for him. It makes us aware of the disdain Drew Oslett feels for Karl Clocker, a disdain he could not afford to have Clocker be aware of. We see his obsession with action, sound, and bright lights as the abnormality it is—something he could not show us, since this obsession is normal for him. Through third-person omniscient we are also able to see Paige in her professional role, working in her office, and can be shown her fear of what is happening to her family, a fear that she would want to play down when she is with them. It allows us to see Karl Clocker's love of *Star Trek*, a love that is based on both the adventure and the morality that the series represents. Because we see this, we can accept his actions at the end of the novel, when he betrays the Network and rescues the Stillwaters. It is exactly the sort of moral action that the crew of the *Enterprise* would elect. No one character could show us these aspects of the different characters, and thus much would be lost in the novel had Koontz chosen an alternative point of view.

He has, however, done one thing in *Mr. Murder* that is unusual in his work. While he has stayed with his customary point of view, he has used both present and past tenses to tell the story. Most of the novel is in the past tense, but whenever the anonymous narrator focuses on Alfie, that chapter is told in present tense. Thus, Chapter 1, which begins with Marty Stillwater listening to his tape recorder and trying to figure out what he meant by saying "I need, I need" over and over again into it, is told in the past tense. However Chapter 2 opens with Alfie in Kansas City, where he has been sent to assassinate someone fingered by the Network, and is told in the present tense. Chapter 3, which focuses on the perspective of Marty's children, is again in the past tense. But Chapter 4, focusing again on Alfie in Kansas City, reverts to the present tense, as does every subsequent chapter that is centered on Alfie and his actions. This shift in tenses is an effective device for maintaining tension throughout the story. Subconsciously it sends the message that we should be very frightened because Alfie exists now, in real time, and could show up in our neighborhoods at any time, just as he does in Marty's suburban, middle-class home.

THEMATIC ISSUES

The influence of the media on human behavior is a key theme in *Mr. Murder*. Television, movies, popular literature, and computer simulations and games all provide models for behavior. When characters seek to explain something to themselves about their lives—the situation they are in, the world around them—they resort to the media for frames of reference. Karl Clocker's frame of reference is *Star Trek*, including the television series, the films, and the books. When Alfie is trying to pacify one of the Stillwaters' neighbors and play down what is going on, he tells him that an obsessed fan is stalking him. The neighbor immediately relates this to a Michael J. Fox film and is satisfied with the explanation. When Paige Stillwater is considering how she will need to act in the face of the threat of Alfie, she decides that she will be like Sigourney Weaver in *Aliens*. When she and Marty are trying to decide where to take a stand against Alfie, they refer to Western films.

Of all the characters, Alfie is the most dependent on the media. When he is trying to complete his life, to become a real person, he takes his image of what that would be from films, ending up in a morass of contradictions. He knows that he must be firm, and also gentle and giving. He knows that he has nothing to fear from death, that heroes are invulnerable, and he also knows that death is a terrible thing. He knows that sexual relationships are fun and joyous, and that they are manipulative and destructive. He knows that children are innocent and good, and that they are corrupt and evil. He understands that women wish to be loved and treated tenderly, and that they wish to be physically and mentally dominated. Alfie has done what small children do, in that he has modeled his behavior on the media, accepting the images he sees there as factual descriptions of how humans should and do interact. And when Alfie's handlers are trying to figure out what went wrong, how they lost control of him, Clocker suggests that it was all the movies and television that caused him to want to change.

Drew Oslett, Alfie's controller, is nearly as dependent in his own way on the media as Alfie is. Oslett loves motion, color, bright lights, and loud noises. It is as though he constantly lives in a Saturday morning children's cartoon and when things quiet down, he is uncomfortable: something is not right. He is constantly in action, watching films, playing with his Game Boy, doing anything to maintain a high level of sensory input. He is very uncomfortable with books, though. He finds them slow and lacking in action, too focused on what people think rather than on what they do. In this he is typical of a pattern in the novel that assigns a love of books to the protagonists, a love of other media to the antagonists.

Martin Stillwater, who is a mystery writer, says of stories that they take the mess of life, with its chaos and unpredictability, and impose on it a sense of order, logic, and meaning. He sees real danger in the visual media, though. He thinks that the combination of its saturation of society and insistence on entertainment values so blurs the distinction between fact and fiction that underlying meaning is all but impossible to arrive at. In both cases—that of stories and that of television and movies—a fictional model is imposed on reality, but there is an essential difference in who is doing this imposing. In the case of literature, it is the reader who interprets a story in such a way that he or she finds meaning in the randomness of life, and for this reason the reader is a key controlling factor. In the case of the visual media, it is the media that impose meaning, since the viewer is not a participant in creating the story. Someone who reads a book must also help to create the book by imagining setting, tone, appearance of characters, and the like. Someone who watches a movie has all of this worked out by the maker of the movie and is just a receptor of that person's imagination. By extension, in considering the media as a whole, popular novels and stories can empower us; they can give us tools with which to shape our experiences, stories to help us make sense of our lives. In contrast, the media, which cannot explore issues and their ramifications in the same way that novels can, give us ways of acting that bear little relationship to reality and that have within them so many internal contradictions that any attempt to follow them as models leads to chaos.

The underlying concept here, then, is that people need models—ways of interpreting the world around them that give it meaning—in order to feel complete in themselves and in their lives, but today's culture no longer provides us with ways that work. When our culture was dependent on the written word, we helped to shape the stories that made sense of our lives. Now that culture is dependent on pictures and sounds, we have become receivers of someone else's vision and are no longer creating the way we interpret our own reality. This leaves us less than whole, makes of us partial people like Alfie, and leads to a very bleak vision of contemporary life. There is a grave danger that, like Alfie, most people will spend their lives as tools of larger forces, controlled by someone else's images of reality, dissatisfied with the lives they have, and at the same time incapable of changing them. There is little to counterbalance this very pessimistic ending to *Mr. Murder* except the suggestion that we must keep on telling stories, attempting to make sense of life as active agents rather than as passive receivers. Then, if we are very lucky and fate as well as our own actions intervenes, we may be able to have fulfilling lives.

ALTERNATIVE READING: THE SOCIOLOGICAL NOVEL

A sociological novel, also known as a thesis novel, "concentrates on the nature, function and effect of the society in which characters live" (Holman and Harmon 1992, 448). It includes within it the serious consideration of issues current in the society—sometimes with the goal of correcting them in specific ways, at other times simply with the goal of exposing them. Classic sociological novels are Harriet Beecher Stowe's *Uncle Tom's Cabin* (1852), with its deeply moving portrait of slaves in pre-Civil War America; Charles Dickens' *Hard Times* (1854), with its vivid descriptions of the plight of the working class in Victorian England; and John Steinbeck's *The Grapes of Wrath* (1939), with its wrenching portrayal of Oklahomans who immigrated to California because of the ravages of the Dust Bowl.

As a sociological novel, *Mr. Murder* raises concerns about the effects on contemporary society of the mass media, of computers and the hidden network they have brought us, and of the shift from a society based on the written word to one based on images and sound. These are concerns that many Americans share. We are, for example, attempting to determine the effect of television on children. Studies suggest that children believe the characters they see on television, even the cartoon characters, are real, and are examples of how people act in the real world. If the television characters are violent, then from the child's point of view violence is a normal way for people to act, a natural response. Such modeling is evident in *Mr. Murder*, where Alfie bases his sense of what to do in a given situation on the movies that he has watched. It is also in Drew Oslett's insistence on constant action, because constant action is the norm in the video games and action films he loves. In more subtle ways, such modeling is also evident in Paige Stillwater's desire to be Sigourney Weaver when she needs to be strong and heroic, as well as in the use she and Marty make of Western films as a resource for how to defend themselves against Alfie.

Mr. Murder also illustrates the shift from the media of literacy to the media of images and sounds. Drew Oslett, who as a graduate of Harvard and Princeton might be expected to be a dedicated champion of literacy, of books and their applicability to life, is instead a champion of action, adventure, and surface stories—tales that link one event after another with no regard for why these events happen or what they suggest about life. The fictions that are developed in written stories demand interaction on the part of the reader, and also have the space to explore character, to consider why people act as they do and what repercussions these actions have on themselves and on society. For this reason, they are often defined as character-driven stories. In contrast, films and television lend themselves poorly to this kind of story. Constraints of time and the difficulty of exploring character through image and sound make these stories plot-driven—that is, they focus on what happens first, what happens after that, and what comes after that, rather than on what happens first, how it affects the characters, how they act in response, how this action affects what will happen next, and so on.

In all times and places, people have told stories to help themselves make sense of their lives and their fates. Sociologically, we are in a time when the means by which we tell stories has changed, moving from the written word to the world of images and sound. We do not yet know what effect this will have on us as a culture. Perhaps the media will bring us together in a global world, a world of shared cultures. Perhaps the media will leave us with a culture so barren that we would be better off with none. Perhaps computers and technology, in their enormous power, will bring us wonders undreamed of. But perhaps they will also bring us controls undreamed of. Finally, *Mr. Murder* leaves us with this quandry: we have created a very dangerous world, and we may not have the means to control it. We may all end up as Alfie does, creatures who sense a deep loneliness and need in our lives, but who are unable to fill it because of the emptiness of the culture we live in. In this way, *Mr. Murder* is a sociological novel that concerns itself with some of the most significant issues of our time and leaves us with no easy answers.

10

Dark Rivers of the Heart
(1994)

Dark Rivers of the Heart is in many ways a new approach for Dean Koontz. With its use of humor as an integral part of the story, it is his most relaxed work to date, and its lack of ultimate closure makes it also the most realistic. Koontz has always known how to write books in which adventure and the breathless question of what will happen next keep the reader turning pages until late into the night. Now he has added to this a critique of society in the computer age that tells us a good deal about ourselves and leaves us with no easy answers. In this way, the novel works on two different levels: it is popular fiction, in that it is highly entertaining and can be read as simply a fine adventure story concerned with the use of technology, and it is also a mainstream novel that presents us with unanswered and uncomfortable questions about the way our world works.

In looking at the difference between fiction that is considered to be "popular" and fiction that is considered to be "literature," a good, broad definition is that "popular" fiction reinforces our preconceived notions of how the world works; we leave this fiction reassured that things are as we have thought them to be. In contrast, "literature" forces us to question our preconceived notions and we leave it with the uncomfortable sense that things may not be as we thought, that we must go back and examine our assumptions of who and what we are, both as individuals and as a society. In *Dark Rivers* Koontz has created a story that works on both levels, entertaining us and at the same time leaving us feeling uneasy after we close the book.

GENRE

Most of Dean Koontz's books overlap genres. Any one work may contain elements of the mystery, horror novel, science fiction, and so on (see Chapter 2), and for this reason Koontz considers himself to be a writer of suspense fiction, a genre that encompasses many genres. However, one of his most recent novels, *Dark Rivers of the Heart* (1994), is an exception, since it is a pure example of the technothriller. This is a very recent genre, and most critics consider the first of the technothrillers to be Tom Clancy's *The Hunt for Red October* (although technothriller author Stephen Coonts makes a good case for Edward L. Beach's 1955 submarine tale *Run Silent, Run Deep*). The defining characteristic of the technothriller is its treatment of technology—that is, of weapons, equipment, and tools. These take on a life of their own and almost become characters in their own right. Readers are as interested in the descriptions of the gadgets involved as they are in the characters using them. Rosenberg and Herald say of this genre, "Until the enormous changes in eastern Europe at the end of the decade, the enemy was usually the Soviets and a common theme was the 'good Russian' in some way conveying superior Soviet technology to the United States. More recent technothrillers use the Middle East and South America for settings. The war on drugs is also developing as an important facet of technothrillers" (1991, 114). In *Dark Rivers*, Dean Koontz has worked an interesting variation on this pattern by making both the good and bad characters Americans, and the contest between them one of who will be able to dominate the world of computers and cyberspace and by doing so, control the future of America.

PLOT DEVELOPMENT

In *Dark Rivers of the Heart*, the original situation (see Chapter 3 for a definition) is that Spencer Grant is going to the Red Door cocktail lounge, looking for a waitress he had met there the night before, Valerie Keene. Grant spends a lot of time in bars, not because he is a heavy drinker but because he is seeking an audience, someone he can tell his story to who will have forgotten about it the next morning. The story consists of a partial memory from his past that is filled with terror. He cannot come to the end of the memory, though, and he hopes that the telling and retelling of it will help him remember its conclusion. While he usually does not return to the same bar, in this case he does so because he felt an immediate bonding with Keene, and he thinks that she felt the same way about him.

The initial plot complication is the fact that Valerie does not come to work at her usual time. When Spencer gets to the bar she is already an hour late, and this is most unlike her—in the two months that she has been at the Red Door she has never been late before. Furthermore, she doesn't answer her phone. Complications build as Spencer goes to her house to see if she is there (he knows where it is because he had surreptitiously followed her home the night before), and he finds it emptied out: no furniture, no clothing, and clearly no one still living there. While he is in the house, it is attacked by what he thinks is a SWAT team. Not wanting to be found uninvited in someone else's house, he escapes, using the training he has as an ex-army ranger. Later, thinking about what has happened, he wonders who the men who attacked the house really were: some of the things they did do not jibe with their being a legitimate SWAT team. And, of course, he wonders what Valerie has done, that a group like this is seeking her.

Spencer returns home and tries to track Valerie through his computer. At one point he was a policeman on the Los Angeles computer task force, and so he knows a great deal about computers and how to use them, legally and illegally, to access information. He discovers that Valerie Keene is apparently a person without a past, someone who has existed for only a few months. Intrigued, he tries to track her through her landlord, who turns out to be a mysterious Asian named Louis Lee. Lee confirms Spencer's guess that the SWAT team was an illegal group, and puts him in touch with Valerie's coworker. The coworker thinks that Valerie once worked in Las Vegas, perhaps as a dealer in the casinos, and Spencer then pursues this lead, discovering her under another identity. He goes to Las Vegas, and while he is there, he realizes he is being followed. In attempting to escape his followers he drives out into the desert, where he is caught in a terrible storm and carried away by a flash flood racing through an arroyo. He is rescued by Valerie, who as it turns out knew that he had followed her home and, in turn, followed him home, placing a transmitter on his truck. She needs to know who he is and why he followed her, because a number of people are looking for her.

Through Valerie, Spencer learns that she—and now Spencer because of his connection to her—is being sought by a clandestine group and that the group reaches high into the government, under the leadership of Thomas Summerton, deputy assistant attorney general. The group makes use of computer technology, satellite hookups, and the like to control and destroy those they deem harmful. A conservative, paramilitary organization, they are after Valerie because she was married to Summerton's son, Danny. Both she and Danny were computer experts, and Danny created a program for his father that allowed him total access to business, government, and individual files. When Danny realized the purpose for which his father was using the program and tried to stop him, Thomas Summerton had his son killed. Valerie escaped, and now the agency is after her. It also wants to find Spencer to learn what his connection with Valerie is, and what Spencer knows about the agency's activities.

Spencer and Valerie together are now on the run from the agency, making use of Valerie's considerable computer skills to save themselves. They have also fallen in love, and Valerie is determined to help Spencer resolve the issue of his partial memories. They decide that they must return to his childhood home in Colorado in order to do this.

While all of this is going on, further complications occur when the leader of the team following Valerie and Spencer, Roy Miro, meets and falls in love with an ex-Las Vegas show girl who now is responsible for the computer taping of all the communications regarding casino activities that routinely take place in Las Vegas. She uses the knowledge she gains in this way at first for economic advantage and later for political advantage. She and Roy share a vision of a world of perfection, and they spend much time discussing ways to eliminate imperfection by killing off all the imperfect human beings in society.

In his search for Valerie and Spencer, Miro has learned that Spencer is the child of Steven Ackblom, a famous artist who was also a serial killer (he displayed his victims in underground tableaux). Ackblom killed his wife and forty other women before being discovered by his then fourteen-year-old son when Ackblom was in the midst of a torture killing. The son shot him, and it is this event that stays with Spencer as a partial memory: What part of it has he forgotten? Why did he forget it? Can he recover it?

Miro decides that Spencer is tormented by his past and will inevitably return to the family home in Colorado to make sense of it. Miro goes to the prison for the criminally insane where Steven Ackblom is serving a life sentence, and by using false papers, removes him from the facility. Miro believes that his best chance of getting information from Spencer is to confront him with his father, Steven.

In the climax, Valerie and Spencer return to Spencer's childhood home, not realizing that the clandestine team is there waiting for them. They enter the underground chamber where Steven Ackblom did his killing, and Spencer recovers his memories of the night he shot his father. He is then confronted by his father and Roy, and in questioning Steven, Spencer learns that he had no part in the death of that evening's victim, as his father tried to assert he did. He is thus freed of the fear and guilt of the past and so can love Valerie and carry on with his life. At this point Roy shoots Valerie, wounding her but not killing her; Steven Ackblom shoots Roy, paralyzing him but not killing him; and Spencer shoots Steven, killing him. Spencer says that he has done this to avenge his mother, and Valerie tells him that if he had not killed Steven, she would have. Valerie and Spencer then escape the trap set by the agency, again through the use of Valerie's computer skills.

Finally, in the denouement we learn that Roy has survived, and that he and Eve have put into place a plan whereby she is to, within the next few years, take over as president of the United States, something made possible by Roy's connections with the agency and Eve's use of the knowledge she has gained from monitoring computer tapes. Valerie and Spencer have escaped from the agency and joined a resistance group made up of people with superb computer skills. The group is dedicated to disrupting the programs of Miro's group and seeing to it that ultimately they have no power because their information is interrupted and, therefore, unreliable. Thus, one group is attempting to take over by use of computer technology and another is attempting to foil them by use of computer technology. Valerie and Spencer are expecting a baby, and other characters see this as a sign of hope for the future, a sign that the resistance will triumph.

CHARACTER DEVELOPMENT

There are two major protagonists in *Dark Rivers*, Spencer Grant and Valerie Keene, as well as two minor protagonists, Valerie's friend Rosie and Louis Lee, who helps Valerie and Spencer.

Spencer Grant is a round, well-developed character of whom we know a great deal. The traumatic events of his childhood are described in detail, and their effect on his later life is made clear: he is haunted by incomplete memories and by his need to come to terms with a strong feeling of guilt that he does not understand. His mother died when he was eight and his father is in a prison for the criminally insane. Spencer has been an army ranger, a Los Angeles policeman, and a member of its computer crime task force. Although he is only in his thirties he has retired from the police and now amuses himself by experimenting with his computers and the various types of access he can achieve through them. He is in the process of erasing himself from official records because he feels that he may at some point want to disappear, although this feeling is nebulous and not well defined—something he just may want to do at some point for reasons that he is uncertain of. Quiet and a loner, he is proud of his self-control. His only real attachment, at the opening of the novel, is with an abused dog named Rocky, whom he has rescued from the pound. (Like all of Dean Koontz's dogs, Rocky is a dog that even dog haters would love to own.) Like Alfie of *Mr. Murder*, Spencer says that he is searching for a life, by which he means that he needs to feel like a complete human being. In the case of Spencer, this would mean that he had full access to his memories and had come to terms with the undefined guilt he feels.

When Spencer meets Valerie Keene, it is a case of love at first sight, and he persists in tracking her down because he feels that she can help him find the life he seeks. He has already adopted one new identity in his life, since the name he has now is not his original one. His father's crimes were so notorious and generated so much publicity that he changed his name, choosing for new names two from the world of the classic movies, "Spencer" after Spencer Tracy and "Grant" after Cary Grant. Thus, like Alfie, Spencer loves movies and bases something of who he is on the films he has seen.

Finally, Spencer is an interesting character in that he is not intimidated by the fact that Valerie's computer skills are superior to his own. Instead, he is a contemporary hero who is able to work as an equal with the women in his life. Spencer is a dynamic character, since at the beginning of the novel he is striving to come to terms with his past and with who he is. By the end of the novel he has achieved this: he now knows that his memory block concerns the death of one of his father's victims, and that his feeling of guilt is based on the fact that his father has convinced him that he, Spencer, is in part responsible for the death. When he confronts his father in the climax, he learns that this is not true; it is simply another example of the father's psychopathology, and his father was the only murderer.

The second major protagonist is Valerie Keene, another rounded character, although her background is given in less detail than Spencer's.

Also in her thirties, Valerie is a computer software designer who specialized in creating video games. She was married to Danny Summerton, the only child of Deputy Assistant Attorney General Thomas Summerton. Danny was also a designer of computer software, and created a program called Mama, one that had the capability of accessing virtually any information. We know very little of Danny except that when he realized his father was using the program for political control, he attempted to stop him and as a result was killed by his father's agents. Valerie was also supposed to be killed—she has far too much information about Mama to be allowed to live—but she escaped the initial attack and has been on the run from Summerton's group for over a year.

Valerie is brave, resourceful, and intelligent. Her knowledge of computers and her ability to use them to protect herself are nothing short of awesome. Reversing the usual male-female roles in thrillers, it is she who is the most knowledgeable character and who is responsible for her own and Spencer's survival. She is a dynamic character only to the extent that, through her relationship with Spencer, she realizes that although Danny is dead, she will be able to love other people in her life. Doing so will be no denial of what she felt for Danny; indeed, it may well be a celebration of those feelings. Other than this change, she remains the same throughout the novel.

Two minor protagonists are Valerie's coworker Rosie, who provides Spencer with a clue that helps him to find her, and Louis Lee, the man who is apparently head of the resistance movement. Rosie is basically a plot device, someone who exists to help the story along rather than for any intrinsic reason of her own. But Lee plays a more significant role since he makes possible the alternative use of technology explored in the novel—that of technology used for society's benefit. He is a relatively flat character; all we know of him is that he has escaped from many of the political hell-holes of contemporary history, including the fall of Saigon, and that those around him look upon him as a hero. His experience has led him to distrust all governments, and he tells Spencer that his loyalties lie with individuals rather than with organizations. It is within his resistance group that Spencer and Valerie find sanctuary. Lee is a static character, remaining the same throughout the work.

One other protagonist is the police captain Harris Descoteaux, who was Spencer's superior in the LAPD. Very little information is given about him other than that he is a good policeman and a good person, but he has the misfortune of creating a negative impression on Roy Miro, who retaliates by destroying his career through planted evidence. There is a terrifying scene in which members of the agency assault his home in a supposed drug raid. Everything he owns is seized under federal property-forfeiture statutes and he is put in prison. Descoteaux is a minor character and therefore little background information is given on him. However, he is a dynamic character in that he comes to see the world of authority and power very differently, as a result of his experiences, from how he did at the beginning of the novel. Where he was once very doubting of anyone's claiming to be innocent and saying he or she was framed, he now knows that framing can and does happen.

Dark Rivers has as its major antagonist Roy Miro, a round but static, non-changing character. Like Steven Ackblom, Roy is also a psychopathic killer. He goes through life seeking out anyone who seems to him to live a less than perfect life, and when he kills such people he is convinced that he is being a good Samaritan, releasing them from the pain of living. His idea of a perfect world is one in which everyone is identical to everyone else, there is only one sex, and "human beings reproduced by discreet parthenogenesis in the privacy of their bathrooms—though not often" (94). There would be only one skin color, a pale blue, and no one would be too dumb or too smart. He believes that it is imperative that the state be powerful, that only in that way can progress be achieved. He thinks the power of the state is based on the degree of people's dependency on it—the more dependent they are, the stronger the state—thus, individualists are a threat to society. Miro is one of the few people in the agency who understands that its real goal is absolute power. Most of the other members think that they are working for an orthodox government agency engaged in orthodox activities. We know very little about Miro other than his goal of a perfect world, but he is so bizarre that he feels fully developed. He is a static character who ends the novel as he began it, working for the agency and committed to creating the new society.

There are two minor antagonists, Eve Marie Jammer and Thomas Summerton. The gorgeous, ex-showgirl Jammer loves power as much as does Miro, and when the two meet, it is love at first sight. Jammer's background is sketched in enough to make her more than a stock character—she is the illegitimate daughter of Summerton—but the reader has little sense of why she has made the specific choices she has, of what other alternatives were open to her and why she rejected them. She is a static character whose only dynamic characteristic is her falling in love with Miro. But since the two are so similar in their worldview, she gains no insights into herself or into the way the world works from this association, only the validation that comes with agreement.

Thomas Summerton is the novel's symbol of ultimate evil, but he never appears in the novel in his own person: we see him only through the eyes of other people, from the perspectives of Valerie, Roy, and Eve. For these reasons he is a stock character, the ultimate villain whose villainy is beyond explanation and who never changes in his single-minded pursuit of his goals. There are also a number of minor antagonists who are the other operatives and employees of the agency, but these again are stock characters, here to people the stage on which the action occurs rather than to initiate the action.

One specific issue raised by *Dark Rivers of the Heart* is the introduction of the character Harris Descoteaux. He is a captain in the Los Angeles Police Department and was Spencer's superior before he joined the computer task force. But the only thing he does in the novel that relates to Spencer is to give Roy Miro background information on the kind of cop Spencer was. This information could just as easily be gained from records (in fact, most of it already has been), and Miro learns nothing that will help him. The reader understands that Descoteaux thinks Spencer was a good person, but this has already been established in other ways, one of which is the bonding of the dog Rocky with Spencer; if an abused dog trusts a character, then that character must be an okay person. Sometimes the best way of getting at why an author has included a particular scene or character is to imagine the book without them and see what is changed. One significant element in the Miro-Descoteaux meeting is that Descoteaux, in backing up his statement that Spencer could not be involved in anything morally wrong, says that he knows that it would not be possible because Spencer is a man who agonizes over right and wrong. He tells Miro, "Whatever the crime . . . the kind of man you want to be looking for is one who's absolutely certain of his righteousness." He adds, "No one's more dangerous than a man who's convinced of his own moral superiority" (148).

This statement could be a description of Roy Miro, who is absolutely certain of himself and the rightness of everything he does, and he reacts to Descoteaux's comment by deciding to have him killed. Then Miro decides that, no, there are better ways to get back at him. This certainly seems like an extreme reaction to a general statement that is, after all, only Descoteaux's opinion and wasn't even specifically directed at Miro. His reaction to it shows a number of things about him. First, Miro is clearly paranoid, interpreting every statement made in terms of himself. Second, he is clearly powerful—he does not for a moment doubt that he can have Descoteaux killed or destroyed simply for having an opinion that Miro disagrees with. And, of course, Miro turns out to be correct about whether or not he can do this: Descoteaux is destroyed, professionally and personally, even though he is a captain in the police department with an exemplary record. If this can happen to Descoteaux, then it could happen to any one of us. If Miro can take such extreme measures on the basis of a whim, then he and the agency he represents are exceedingly powerful and out of control. Thus, the inclusion of Harris Descoteaux in the story may add little to the plot development, but it is significant in terms of adding evidence to the claim that we have much to fear from rogue agencies such as Miro's group.

SETTING

Dark Rivers of the Heart makes less use of the weather and of natural settings than any of the other Koontz books covered in this Critical Companion. There is a rainstorm when Spencer is first trying to find Valerie, one that helps to hide him from the agency operatives who are assaulting her house. Fog emphasizes the fact that Miro and his men cannot find Spencer because he has laid so many false trails. A snowstorm helps to hide and protect Valerie from the hit men when Danny is killed. But these are one-time events rather than on-going motifs as, for example, lightning is in the novel *Lightning* (see Chapter 6). Good use is made in *Dark Rivers* of the flash flood in the desert, since the flood becomes the rationale for Valerie's meeting with Spencer; if she had not rescued him, he would have died, and without a device such as the storm, she probably would not have approached Spencer, since she has little reason to trust strangers, especially strangers who have followed her home from work late at night.

So far as physical locations are concerned, Spencer first meets Valerie in Los Angeles, a city known for its lack of intimacy and its atmosphere of separateness and loneliness. This is a fine place for a man like Spencer, who up to now has not even fully connected with himself, let alone anyone else, and it is also a convincing place for someone like Valerie to go to ground. The rural Colorado country that Spencer lived in as a boy also works to add credibility to events in the novel, since it is isolated enough that a psychopathic killer might indeed be able to commit crimes there for years without being caught. When the agency operatives move in during the climax, the area's isolation makes it believable that such an event could take place, out of sight of the public, where there would be no one to raise alarms.

Another good use of place is the city of Las Vegas, where Valerie has been working as a dealer. This is a city of thousands of transients who are far more interested in the gambling than they are in one another. A stranger coming into town is the norm rather than an event to be remarked on. It is also a city of enormous clandestine power in the shape of the mob, who are assumed by most people to control the gambling and to use the city for laundering money. Such power makes the power of Summerton and his agency more credible by association: if there can be a secret, powerful group like the mob, why can't there be another powerful group? And finally, the use of Miami in the denouement as the location for the resistance serves two functions: since Miami is known as an international city with international connections, particularly connections with Latin America and its various real-life resistance groups, we are prepared to accept it as the site for this fictional resistance group. At the same time, Miami's beautiful beaches, its sun, and its sand and tropical climate make it seem like paradise, as though perhaps here society really could return to Eden, to a time of innocence when there were no groups such as Summerton's.

The novel's most inspired use of artificial setting is that of technical equipment and weapons, especially the computers and the access they give to cyberspace. Spencer uses his computer expertise to find Valerie. The agency uses its expertise to find Spencer. And both the agency and Valerie make ingenious use of surveillance equipment to track and, in Valerie's case, hide, from one another. One of the delights of the novel is that characters who are being tracked by the use of technology are, in turn, evading their trackers by the use of the same technology. There are fascinating descriptions of computer-generated portraits of Spencer developed from details seen through the rain, of the retrieval of fingerprints by high-tech means and their identification through computers, and of devices such as infinity transmitters, which are undetectable telephone wiretaps that work even when no one is talking on the phone. In the climax, it is Valerie's capture of the satellite *Godzilla*—something that Spencer calls a "death-ray satellite" and that Valerie explains is really "enhanced-laser technology" (466)—that enables them to defeat Miro and his men. Valerie constructs a grid that is essentially a gameboard and shoots down the operatives with molten laser paths when they attempt to come near her and Spencer. Anyone who's played even the simplest computer game cannot help but become involved in the *Godzilla* game, and the fact that computers now do the extraordinary things that they do in real life makes it plausible that there are satellites such as *Godzilla*, that they can be captured by someone knowledgeable enough and desperate enough to work her way into the system, and that they could be used as Valerie has used *Godzilla*.

POINT OF VIEW

Like nearly all of Dean Koontz's novels, *Dark Rivers of the Heart* uses the third-person omniscient point of view. This point of view allows readers to see Spencer's loneliness, something he tells only to drunks, who promptly forget what was said. It allows us to see how utterly wacko Roy Miro really is, something he cannot reveal to the other characters because even he knows that his actions and beliefs would not be accepted. It demonstrates the existence of Louis Lee and the resistance movement, something so secret that the information would not be openly revealed. It shows Valerie's feelings for her first husband and how she thinks of them in terms of her feelings for Spencer, something she would be unlikely to tallk about. The scene in which Harris Descoteaux's house is raided is shown, even though none of the main characters know about it, and so could not report on it. And Eve's relationship to Thomas Summerton, something neither of them would be likely to discuss, is also clarified. Third-person omniscient is ultimately a practical way of giving readers information about different people in different situations and keeping the action of the story clear and understandable.

In addition to omniscient voice, Koontz also uses first person to describe Spencer Grant's partial memories. In first-person point of view, a character relates the events of a story from the I point of view. This is a classic point of view to choose for stories in the hard-boiled detective genre: "I was in my office, deciding whether to open another bill or give it up for the day" might be a standard hard-boiled opening. When first person is used, everything is filtered through the perceptions of the I narrator, and only that perception is known to the reader. Essentially, the reader must interpret the story through the eyes, ears, and personality of the narrator, and must decide how much to trust the narrator. First person is a common choice when the author wants the reader to identify with the narrator and it is effective in describing Grant's memories. The terror he feels in them is shared with the reader and the reader experiences the development of the memories as they grow and become more complete, almost as though the reader were remembering along with Spencer. We are both frightened and intrigued by what we, through Spencer, might remember next.

THEMATIC ISSUES

The major theme of *Dark Rivers of the Heart* is that society is disintegrating, simply falling apart. One of the opening images of the novel is that of a filthy man huddled in a doorway. When Spencer sees him, he thinks of all the mentally ill who roam the streets of American cities, "freed from sanitariums in the name of civil liberties and compassion . . . championed by politicians but untended, an army of the living dead" (7). When Valerie does not show up for work, Spencer imagines her murdered corpse, and even though he knows this is an overreaction, he thinks, "These days, the average American routinely lived in anticipation of sudden, mindless violence" (18).

When he is caught in the agency assault on Valerie's house, Spencer's first reaction is that he is in the middle of a gang war, a daily occurrence in contemporary Los Angeles. When Roy Miro thinks about the city, he reflects on the fact that most of the motorists seem to be drunk or on drugs, and he watches a homeless man pushing a shopping cart full of belongings, "his face expressionless, as if he were a zombie shuffling along the aisles of a Kmart in Hell" (31). Miro believes that the apocalypse is coming and that it is inevitable, that human beings are "drawn to turmoil and self-destruction as inevitably as the earth was drawn to complete its annual revolution of the sun" (33).

It is not only the city of Los Angeles that is seen in this bleak light. Spencer thinks that most government agencies devote their energies to justifying their own existence, rather than doing what they were intended to do. Miro would agree with him, and would add that politicians have so meddled with the Drug Enforcement Agency that it is incapable of fulfilling its mission. He also sees the military services as "confused as to their purpose, underfunded, and moribund" (265). When Miro, still trying to find Spencer, breaks into an average middle-class home, he finds the inhabitants out of work, looking for jobs, and living on welfare, victims of a recession they had no part in creating. Roy thinks about how he will have to be more careful the next time he breaks into a home, that even if he has convincing credentials, a government raid on a private home has become a risky business: "The residents might be anything from child-molesting worshipers of Satan to cohabiting serial killers with cannibalistic tendencies." He adds, "On the cusp of the millennium, some damned strange people were loose out there in fun-house America" (111).

The most damning social comment in *Dark Rivers of the Heart* is its description of the forfeiture laws, which allow the government to seize the goods of private citizens who have not been proven guilty of anything, and who do not even have to be formally charged. The claim is made that such laws, designed to apply only to major drug dealers and members of organized crime, are now being far more generally applied and are becoming an important source of funds for the agencies involved. Harris Descoteaux's brother Darius, a lawyer, tells him that there are now two hundred federal offenses for which forfeiture laws can be applied, and that in one year, they were applied 50,000 times. Readers who take the time to read Koontz's afterword will be even more alarmed at the picture the novel draws of these laws. Koontz tells the reader that his description of these laws and how they work is essentially factual. This image of an America in decay is an ironic one, since it describes an America that has been brought about by our best intentions. Valerie says, "By insisting on a perfect world, we've opened the door to fascism" (304), by which she means that in our attempt, as a society, to fix everything for everyone, we have let loose unlimited government power.

When one looks at the alternative proposed by the novel to the present state of society, the picture remains bleak. Koontz proposes two basic scenarios: fascism and revolution. That is, either things will remain as they are, with political agencies gaining more and more power over the individual citizen, or individual citizens will band together to take control of cyberspace, the new source of power in today's world. Should this happen, Koontz provides the reader with no guarantee that this group, in its turn, will handle power well. The novel's final message— its underlying theme—is that the power of technology, a power based as much on knowledge as on force, can be used for great evil and it can be used for great good. If we would have a free society, we had better see to it that decisions on how this power will be used are made by individuals accountable to other individuals, and not by faceless bureaucrats acting through clandestine agencies. It is for this reason that the novel ends without coming to full closure, without reassuring the reader that everything will be all right—that evil will be defeated and we will all be safe in our beds. Maybe evil will be defeated and maybe it won't: the final outcome depends on how we choose to use and control the immense power of modern technology. Like the novel, we have not yet come to closure on this issue.

ALTERNATIVE READING: A FEMINIST ANALYSIS

One way of analyzing literature is through a sociological analysis—that is, a look at what the work reflects of the social currents and the status of various groups at the time the work was written. Sociological analyses focus on specific issues such as the view of economic classes, of the sexes, of races, and so on. A feminist analysis, which is one form of sociological analysis, looks at women's roles—their actions and activities and the value that is placed on them (see Chapter 4). Dean Koontz's novels, especially the later ones, lend themselves to such an analysis because he deliberately creates strong roles for women in his stories, saying that any writer who cannot show women in such roles "can't be writing seriously" (Gorman interview, 41). In *Dark Rivers of the Heart* Koontz many times draws the reader's attention to gender, to the roles we might expect women and men to fill, and then to the roles they actually do fill. He is playing with the reader's expectations so as to create a heightened self-awareness on the part of the reader, to have the reader step back and question how he or she really sees gender in the modern world of supposed equality between the sexes. One way he does this is by presenting men in typically feminine positions, as when the receptionist in an office is described as a big, broad, bald bodyguard (complete with concealed weapon) who is typing at great speed. Watching him, Spencer thinks that if he can use his gun as well as he can type, he is a dangerous man. A skill usually associated with women—typing ability—is correlated with a skill usually reserved for men—the use of weapons. The implication is that such skills may be interchangeable, may be accessible to both men and women.

A reverse example of the same sort occurs when a woman, Nella Shire, is shown in a role typically reserved for men—that of the person who objectifies the opposite sex by seeing them in terms of their physical attributes rather than as complete people. She is forty-five years old and an expert on fingerprints, an area that was until recently a masculine preserve. She has pictures of male body builders in bikini briefs pinned up in her work area, in a scene that parodies what used to be the standard male one of using pictures of scantily clad calendar girls to decorate male workplaces. Nella's male manager insists that she take the pictures down, that leaving them up is an act of sexual harassment. While Koontz is clearly having fun with this example of gender reversal, he uses it to make the point that all people, women as well as men, want to be seen as themselves rather than as collections of specific physical attributes.

A good example of gender stereotyping, of assuming that a person is a particular type of person because of gender and appearance, happens with respect to Eve Marie Jammer. She works in the agency's underground recording center in Las Vegas, overseeing the monitoring of thousands of telephones through taps that are recorded onto laser disks. This is a very sensitive position since what is being done is clearly illegal. Eve is trusted here partly because her father is head of the agency, but also because she is so beautiful that her employers assume she is "barely bright enough to change the laser discs from time to time . . . and call in an in-house technician to repair malfunctioning machines" (160). In actuality, Eve is an extremely intelligent woman who has used her position to amass $5 million in two years. She has traded on the stereotype of the beautiful, dumb woman to lull her employees and, in doing so, has benefited from her wit and abilities. It is another reversal of gender stereotypes that Eve has made most of her money through taking advantage of the details she has overheard regarding corporate-stock manipulations and guaranteed point spreads on rigged national sporting events—two areas that would traditionally be considered incomprehensible to women but that, as Koontz shows through Eve, are hardly gender-based.

The major woman character in *Dark Rivers of the Heart* is the protagonist Valerie Keene. In yet another reversal of gender stereotypes, she rescues the hero when he is trapped by a flash flood rather than the hero's rescuing her. She also has knowledge equivalent to and at times superior to that of the hero. Although he was trained in surveillance techniques as an army ranger, she discovers at once that he is following her and, in turn, she follows him, placing a transmitter on his truck. Unlike Valerie, who spots Spencer, Spencer does not spot Valerie, suggesting that she is better than he is at these techniques. Throughout the novel, it is Valerie who is the voice of wisdom, who understands what is going on and why, and who explains it to Spencer. This is again a case of role reversal; traditionally, it is the male hero who is the source of such knowledge. Even in the small details, Koontz emphasizes role reversal and the inaccuracy of gender expectations. Thus, Valerie is a superb driver, as she demonstrates in a high-speed chase—again a skill considered to be a male attribute. In her professional life Valerie also worked in a field usually thought of as a male field, that of computer software design, where her speciality was developing computer games. It is interesting that it is her being in this nontraditional field that first brought her to the attention of Danny, the man who became her husband, suggesting that women can be in fields thought of as men's fields and still be attractive as women. And, of course, it is Valerie's mastery of computers that allows her to capture a satellite, construct what is basically a computer game around it, and so defeat the agency.

One of the ways feminists describe the world and its present power structure is in terms of the concept of the patriarchy, by which is meant the broad collection of traditional white-male power groups in business, the military, and politics. These groups have retained power for themselves by keeping women and other minorities out of positions that would give them access to power. The term patriarchy refers to this group's tendency to see itself as benevolent and fatherly, acting for the good of all of its children, namely the women and nonwhites in society. When Valerie takes on the agency, she is taking on the patriarchy. It is interesting that of the agency operatives who work in the field, none are women and none are minorities. She is also taking on a real father, since Thomas Summerton is her late husband Danny's father. And he is as devastating to his real child as the patriarchy is to its symbolic children: he has Danny killed when Danny aspires to power that would challenge his father. There is also some indication of role reversal in the fact that Summerton's daughter Eve succeeds where her half-brother Danny failed, in that she is able to wrest at least some power from the father. However, she is using power in the same ways that he is, and we cannot know if he would have her killed too if she were the direct challenge to him that Danny was. Finally, among the characters who join the resistance in the novel are its only minorities, a designation that includes women as well as racial and ethnic groups. Valerie's friend Rosie is half Vietnamese and half African American, Louis Lee is Chinese and Harris Descoteaux is African American. If the old America is based on white male power, the potential new America in the form of the resistance will be based on multiethnic, female, and male power.

In all of these ways, then, Dean Koontz makes use of traditional gender roles and stereotypes, as well as of feminist concepts such as that of the patriarchy, to suggest that if there is to be a world of freedom from hidden dictatorships for everyone, it will also be a world of equality, of shared power and of shared access for each gender and all races.

Intensity
(1995)

A typical Dean Koontz book is very long, with multiple story lines, a large cast of characters, an extended time frame, and elements from a number of different literary genres. So much for what is typical. Koontz readers who come to *Intensity* will certainly not be faced with the sort of book they might have expected to find. Instead of a weighty, 400- to 500-page book, they will be holding one that is a rather tidy 300 pages; instead of balancing the details of many simultaneous story lines, they will be following only one story line; instead of becoming involved with a large number of characters, they will be focusing on two main figures; instead of a story that takes place over a sustained period of time, they will be holding their breaths through one that covers a total of only twenty-four hours; instead of a work that crosses different genres, they will be in the world of the pure suspense novel; and finally, in terms of his skills as a wordsmith, they will be in what is to date Dean Koontz's best novel.

Koontz's mastery of the written word has never been better. It is as though the simplicity of the plot has led him to a simplicity of language that, in its pared-down sharpness, adds to the intensity of the title and the story line. Some few examples are his description of silence that "drifted down like a snowfall" (18), his use of the term "hot phase" (54) to describe a psychopath out on a kill, and his vivid image of "stark white bones of lightning" (102) to describe a thunderstorm in the redwoods.

GENRE

As a general rule, any one of Dean Koontz's books includes in it elements of many genres, combining mystery, horror, science fiction, and
so on (see Chapter 2), but *Intensity* is an exception. This is a work of
pure suspense that makes fine use of the race-against-the-clock device
that is classic to this genre. In terms of overall category, *Intensity* fits into
the psychopathic killer subgenre begun by John Fowles with *The Collector*
(1963) and brilliantly developed by Thomas Harris in *The Silence of the
Lambs* (1988). In this subgenre, a man who appears outwardly normal
has a crazed inner fantasy world centered on the capture of young
women. He never perceives these women as real, as having separate lives
outside of his fantasies of them. The terror of such novels lies in the
women's desperate attempts to force their captors to see them as people
like them, as people who exist apart from the fictional world the psychopath has created for them. An underlying assumption of such works
is that if the psychopath could see his victim as being like himself he
could let the victim go. A second underlying assumption is that such
recognition is not possible for the psychopath—if it were, he would not
have taken the victim captive in the first place—and therefore, in the
absence of outside help, the victim is doomed. Whether or not that outside help will appear is the determining factor in what will be the ultimate outcome. Sometimes, as in *The Collector*, there will be no outside
help; sometimes, as in *The Silence of the Lambs*, that help arrives. The fact
that both of these outcomes are equally likely adds to the tension of this
type of suspense novel.

PLOT DEVELOPMENT

In *Intensity*, the original situation (see Chapter 3 for a definition) is that
Chyna Shepherd, a twenty-six-year-old psychology student, is going
with her friend and classmate Laura Templeton to stay at Laura's family
home for the weekend. Chyna is welcomed by Laura's mother and father, and feels very much at home in their Victorian farmhouse.

The initial plot complication comes when, later in the evening, Chyna
cannot sleep; as a child she was dragged by her mother from one unsta-
ble household to another, and as a result the adult Chyna slowly accus-
toms herself to new places. She is sitting by her unmade bed when she

hears a scream, followed by someone moving in the house. She starts to investigate the sounds but then realizes that whoever is moving through the rooms is coming toward her. She hides under the bed, as she so often did in her troubled, abusive childhood. At this point the intruder enters the room and examines it, even opening the closet to make sure that it is as uninhabited as it seems. Because Chyna has not yet felt comfortable enough to even unpack, the intruder finds no evidence of her presence. He goes out, leaving drops of blood behind him. Chyna listens for him to leave the house, and then goes to the Templetons' bedrooms. She finds both of the parents dead, and a violated Laura who has been bound and badly hurt, but who is still alive. Chyna then discovers that the phone lines have been cut, and while she is trying to work out a way to get help for her friend, the intruder returns. He gathers up Laura and takes her out to his large, old motor home. Chyna sneaks aboard the home, determined to rescue Laura, and then realizes that Laura is now dead. She also discovers a second body in the closet of the motor home, arranged in a tableau. The killer, Edgler Vess—does not realize that Chyna is on board. Her plan now is to wait for her chance to get away, and then call the police.

It seems that Chyna has found her chance when Vess stops for gas at a convenience store and Chyna is able to slip, unseen, out of the motor home. She goes into the store but before she can do anything, she realizes that Vess is coming in behind her. With no time to explain anything to the clerks, she says, "Please don't let him know I'm here" (72) and disappears between the aisles, hiding once again. Vess begins talking with the clerks, alternating between normality and the surreal in his conversation. At one point he tells them that he keeps a fifteen-year-old girl captive in his basement, ripening her, and he even shows them a picture that he claims is of the girl. Then he takes out a gun and shoots both of the clerks, carefully counts out the money for his purchases, places it on the counter and leaves the store. After Vess has left Chyna comes out of hiding and finds that here too, the phone lines have been cut and there is no way for her to call for help. At this point she finds the picture of the young girl and realizes that the girl is in all probability real and being held captive. Chyna feels that she must do something to try to save the girl, and when Vess leaves, she takes one of the dead clerk's cars and follows the motor home so that, if nothing else, she will at least know where to send the police, if and when she can contact them.

Vess now detours through a national redwood forest, still unaware of Chyna. Complications build when, deep into the forest, Chyna realizes that she will soon be out of gas. She decides to stage an accident that will force Vess to stop and investigate, and at that point see if she can stow away in the motor home once again and so discover where it is that he lives. She pulls ahead of him and a few miles later, puts her plan into motion, wrecking her car in such a way that it blocks the highway. She leaves the scene and moves in among the trees, waiting for Vess to come upon the accident. While she is waiting, coastal elk appear, gliding among the redwoods. Their presence here, so far from the coast, is most unusual, and Chyna, at first mistaking them for angels, sees them as emblems of hope and protection. Her plan works out exactly as she had envisioned it, and she boards the motor home. This time, however, Vess sees her doing so. He says nothing, deciding to wait and see what it is this woman is doing. (His first assumption is that she is in shock because of the accident and has wandered into the home because it is the nearest shelter. He is looking forward to her reaction when she discovers Laura's corpse.)

Vess drives on to his home in Oregon. Chyna leaves the motor home, still thinking that her presence is unknown, and enters Vess's house, where she finds that he does indeed have a girl captive in his cellar, a special chamber filled with dolls. She promises to save the girl and at this point, Vess knocks her out, chains her to a chair in the kitchen, and tells her that he will be back to have psychotic fun with her (the implication is that he will rape and torture her) and that he will do so in the presence of Ariel, the fifteen-year-old captive. Vess subsequently leaves, explaining to Chyna that he needs to carry on with his normal daily life, one that serves as a cover for his activities, and that he will be back in six hours. With much hard work, creativity, and ingenuity, Chyna succeeds in freeing herself and then Ariel while Vess is gone, fending off in the process a pack of dobermans who have been trained to kill. Again Chyna finds that Vess has left her with no way to communicate to the outside world (there are phone jacks, but no telephones), and so she and Ariel leave in the motor home, their only source of transportation.

The climax occurs when Chyna sees a police patrol car as she is driving and flags it down, only to find that the driver is Edgler Vess—he is, of all things, a policeman. Chyna rams the police car with the motor home. She and Ariel attempt to escape into the forest, with Vess following and gaining on them. As a result of the ramming of the police car there is now gasoline spilled all over the roadway and Chyna manages to set fire to it with a lighter that she's carrying as a weapon of last resort.

Vess is caught in the flames and dies, a human torch still attempting to reach Ariel and Chyna.

In the denouement, Chyna has gained guardianship of Ariel and there is a strong sense that Ariel will overcome the great psychic damage Vess's captivity has done to her. Chyna has changed her major from psychology to literature. She and Ariel spend long days on the shore of San Francisco Bay as Ariel slowly heals and Chyna comes to the conclusion that caring about and for one another is our purpose for existing.

CHARACTER DEVELOPMENT

There are only two major characters in *Intensity*, the protagonist or heroine Chyna Shepherd and the antagonist or villain Edgler Vess. There are also two minor characters, Anne Shepherd, Chyna's mother, who appears only in flashbacks, and the imprisoned Ariel. Of these four the most well-rounded character is Chyna. We know a great deal about her childhood with a psychotic mother who took as lovers a series of sociopaths and deviants, people who lived as though violence were the only means of staying alive. Through these experiences Chyna has learned the basic survival techniques that sustain her when Vess is holding her captive. She has also learned that she has only herself to rely on when in danger, that the authorities around her, represented by her mother, will further endanger her rather than rescue her. In saving Ariel, Chyna applies these lessons and at the same time, helps someone in ways that she herself would like to have been helped as a child.

When we first meet the adult Chyna, she is studying for a master's degree in psychology, with the goal of understanding psychopathology, and plans to earn a doctorate in criminology. She spends a good deal of time going back over the events of her childhood, and in particular, of the actions of her beautiful mother. One scene she revisits many times is the thrill murder of an older couple by her mother and the mother's lover that took place when Chyna was seven. Her mother forced her to watch the deaths, saying to her, "We're different than other people, baby. . . . You'll never understand what freedom really means if you don't watch this" (12). On the evidence of her flashbacks and her college studies, Chyna has spent her adult life attempting to understand her mother. The fact that Chyna is a dynamic or changing character is established when she realizes that there is no understanding Anne, that Anne was as Anne chose to be, just as Edgler Vess is as he has chosen to be. It is at this point that Chyna abandons the study of psychology and becomes a literature major. She has accepted that evil exists in and of itself, and that the best that human beings can do is to protect one another in the face of this knowledge, just as she has protected Ariel.

The second major character is Edgler Vess. He too is a well-rounded character, although we know less about him and his background than we do about Chyna. Vess is a classic psychopath who kills his victims for the sheer pleasure of inflicting pain. He believes that he is motivated by his commitment to intensity of feeling, both physical and mental, and that it is only this intensity that allows a person to be truly alive. Like many psychopaths who see themselves as superior, he believes that he is on the verge of a transformation to a superhuman state, one that will be brought about by his actions rather than by divine intervention "because he has already chosen to live like a god—without fear, without remorse, without limits" (62). He has the typical psychopathic history of torturing and killing animals as a child and then moving on to people, murdering his parents when he was nine and then, two years later, his grandmother. He describes himself as "a homicidal adventurer" (176), but Chyna sees him as only a man "living at one extreme end of the spectrum of human cruelty, but nonetheless only a man" (184). Koontz provides no easy excuses for Vess in terms of giving the reader justification for what he is. When Chyna asks him if he was abused as a child he assures her that on the contrary, he was a loved and even an indulged child. There is no "understanding" Edgler Vess—a thoroughly evil person. The irony here is that according to conventional wisdom it is Chyna, with her abusive childhood, who should be the psychopath rather than Vess, with his normal, loving upbringing. Unlike Chyna, Vess is a static character, since he dies as he lived, glorying in pain.

Of the minor characters, the most significant never appears in the novel as a living person, but only in flashbacks. This is Anne, Chyna's mother, a very beautiful woman who saw violence as glamorous and romantic. Chyna describes her to Laura at the time of the double murders: "I can see her standing there . . . , so ravishing . . . , glorious . . . , like a goddess from another world" (13). She lived with a series of violent men, gun and drug runners, and through her, Chyna witnessed at least three murders. Anne is basically a flat character, since the reader is given no information on her background or on how she came to be enthralled with violence. We do not even know who Chyna's father was, nor why Anne chose to keep the girl with her. Laura asks Chyna if she will ever see Anne again and Chyna says that she would like to, so as to try to understand her, but she adds that it is unlikely, since she has no idea where Anne is. She thinks it very likely that Anne is either in jail or dead, telling Laura, "You can't live like that and hope to grow old" (13). Anne's presence hovers over the book, providing a paradoxical element of optimism in that Chyna has lived through the horror of Anne, and so perhaps she will live through the horror of Edgler Vess, too— she is accustomed to psychopaths.

The fourth character in *Intensity*, Ariel, is a very beautiful fifteen-year-old girl who has been kept captive by Vess for a year when the book opens. He has killed both her parents and has tortured her younger brother to death, probably in Ariel's presence. He is keeping her to "ripen" her for himself, with the implication that when she matures (she is, we are told, almost there) he will rape and torture her as he does his other victims. Meanwhile, he delights in telling her the details of his crimes, even going so far as to give her before and after polaroid pictures of the victims. We do not know how Ariel initially responded to Vess, but when we meet her in the novel, she is in a state of catatonic detachment. Chyna recognizes that in response to the daily horror of her life, Ariel has retreated into an imaginary world where no one can touch her, a protective response that Chyna herself resorted to at various times when she was living with her mother. By the end of the novel Ariel has become a dynamic character, since she has moved from the catatonic state to one where she can write, "I want to live" (307).

SETTING

Intensity is set in California, in the wine country of Napa valley. The majority of the settings used here are the man-made ones of homes and temporary homes, with two significant exceptions, that of the redwood forest and, in the denouement, the ocean. The story opens at the Templeton home, a large, rambling Victorian house that has been in the family for three generations. It is the essence of home, a place of safety and serenity, and the contrast between the house and the events that happen in it is particulary stark, heightening the horror of Vess's murder of the Templeton family. Vess's motor home, another artificial setting, is old, claustrophobic, and with its corners, alcoves, and closets, much like a maze in which one might trap an animal, heightening the reader's fear of what will happen to Chyna once she is inside. However, Vess's house could be any house; there is nothing in the least unusual about it, except for the basement, Ariel's prison. This room is completely soundproofed and filled with dolls that Vess brings to Ariel after each of his killings. The very ordinariness of the house, contrasted with what is in the basement, raises the level of horror: this could be anyone's house, ours or our neighbors. Maybe Edgler Vess really does exist, just around the corner. The use of the dolls as a part of the setting is particularly horrifying, since these should signify the innocent days of childhood but instead, they signify pain and death.

The novel's two natural settings are both sources of peace and spiritual renewal. The first is the redwood forest, an extraordinary place that is described in terms of grace and salvation. When Chyna first enters the grove of trees, she experiences it as a place of safety, "a fortress erected against all the rage of the world" (111), and she senses that she is not alone. She sees what she believes to be angels in the redwoods, and then comes to recognize the angels as a herd of coastal elk, huge, beautiful creatures who approach her, lift their heads, and stare directly at her. Their presence here is magical: they are much farther from the coast than they could reasonably be and, because they are timid by nature, they would surely never approach this closely to a human being. Seeing them gives Chyna the strength to continue with her plan of stowing herself on board the motor home, although when Vess sees them, he reacts differently. To him the elk are ghostly rather than angelic, and he is uneasy that they show no fear of him. In their most unusual appearance in these woods, there is a suggestion that something in nature has taken notice of the likes of Edgler Vess and that in the coming confrontation with him, Chyna may have support beyond her own resources. This suggestion is reinforced when Chyna is chained in Vess's kitchen, on the verge of dispair, and one of the elk appears to her again, staring at her through the window, giving her the courage to go on.

The second use of natural setting is at the end of the novel, at a beach in San Francisco. Here Chyna and Ariel spend many hours, with Ariel staring out at the water and standing in the surf. At this beach Chyna meets a man and his son who subsequently become friends with her and Ariel, forming a sort of family, and it is then that Ariel begins to come out of her catatonic state. Thus, the natural world is seen as a place of peace and healing, and, for Ariel, a return to the human race.

POINT OF VIEW

Like nearly all of Dean Koontz's novels, *Intensity* uses the third person omniscient point of view. This allows the reader to see into the minds of both Chyna Shepherd and Edgler Vess, and Koontz uses it to set up specific contrasts. Thus, when Chyna is in the redwood forest and sees the coastal elk, they appear to her as angels, but when Vess sees these same elk, his reaction to their beauty is that killing them would give him great pleasure. In these differing reactions it becomes clear that Shepherd and Vess are indeed the novel's poles of opposition, with Shepherd in the traditional hero role, Vess in the traditional villain role. Being inside their minds in this way also helps to illuminate Koontz's contention that evil cannot be explained, that it simply is. Chyna's reaction to the elk is as purely instinctive as is Vess's; she is a good person despite her childhood, and he is an evil person despite his.

Another advantage of the third person omniscient point of view in *Intensity* is its ability to heighten the tension by showing what each character knows or does not know. When Chyna is hidden for the second time in Vess's motor home, she believes that he is unaware of her presence. However, because the reader has access to Vess's thoughts as well as to Chyna's, the reader knows that he is well aware of her being on board and that he is amused by this situation in which fate has presented him with a ready-made victim. This increases the suspense, since the reader now knows that Chyna cannot possibly take Vess by surprise, as she had intended to do. Were the story told only from Chyna's point of view, this particular source of fear would be missing from the story.

In the same way, third person omniscient allows the reader to understand the meaning of Chyna's words when she encourages herself with the phrase, "Chyna Shepherd, untouched and alive" (120). We know that this is a prayer left over from her childhood, one that served to protect her then and that perhaps will protect her now. However, when Vess hears the same words, he has no idea what they refer to. They sound to him like a mysterious code and he, who is afraid of nothing, suddenly feels that there is something supernatural and ominous about Chyna. This is in turn a very effective use of foreshadowing, since Chyna's childhood prayer will help her to survive, just as it did when she was with Anne, and Vess is quite right to see her as ominous, since she will bring about his death. Were the story told from Vess's point of view, we would not understand the meaning of Chyna's prayer; were it told from Chyna's point of view, we would not know how Vess interprets the prayer. In each case, the story would lose in terms of its suspenseful buildup.

THEMATIC ISSUES

In *Intensity*, the theme that is specifically stated, not once but a number of times, is that we do have control over our fates, that often we can choose whether or not we will be victims. Chyna first learns this as a child, when she initiates the protective action of hiding from her mother's violent friends, and she acts on it again when, at age sixteen, she leaves her home and mother. Ariel also acts on this knowledge, by choosing to go into a catatonic state in order to escape Vess. When she does this, he becomes intrigued. Ariel is Vess's only long-term captive, and it is likely that he has let her live as long as he has because of the challenge she poses. It is clear that Ariel can to some extent control her catatonic behavior since, in a scene that is a triumph of tension and suspense, she breaks out of the state long enough to help Chyna free both herself and Ariel. Another point that Koontz makes a number of times in the novel is that evil is both inexplicable and real. It is also, Chyna says, inexcusable, a concept that fits well with the theme that we can control our fates. Thus, Vess may not have chosen to have a love of pain, but he chooses whether or not to inflict pain on others; we are all, finally, responsible for our actions.

A second underlying theme of *Intensity* is that just as we can determine our own lives, we also have an obligation to help others determine theirs. Chyna feels that she is absolutely obliged to at least try to rescue Ariel, that the defining characteristic of what it is to be human is the quality of caring for one another. Koontz is repeating a theme here that has appeared many times in his work, and which is most specifically articulated in *Watchers* (see Chapter 5), a book that ends stating that we are all watchers, charged with watching over and for one another. When Chyna thinks back on how much she risked for a girl she did not know, how reckless it was of her to care so strongly about what happened to the girl, she comes to the realization, "It is the purpose for which we exist. This reckless caring" (308).

ALTERNATIVE READING: A FEMINIST FAIRY TALE

Fairy tales exist as oral stories in all folk literature. They were first put into written form by the brothers Wilhelm and Jakob Grimm (1812), and they follow a pattern of being a prose narrative of the adventures of a hero or heroine who, with supernatural or magical help, overcomes all obstacles and lives happily every after. Feminist readings are a form of sociological interpretation in which the roles of women in a specific work are examined in terms of underlying assumptions about women in society and the roles that are and should be open to them (see Chapter 4 for an extended discussion of feminist analysis). One persuasive reading of *Intensity* is to see it as a feminist fairy tale, in which the role traditionally given to a brave young man who is usually a prince is instead given to a brave young woman who is definitely a commoner.

First, in Koontz's fairy tale, there is a brave heroine, Chyna, who fights against all obstacles to rescue Ariel, a beautiful young maiden imprisoned in the dungeon of an ogre, Edgler Vess. (Note that the name "Edgler" sounds a good deal like "ogre"). In her efforts to rescue the maiden, the heroine must face many challenges. Chyna confronts the first of these when she must overcome her fear and go into the lair of the ogre while he himself is there, and she must do this not once but three times, since she goes twice into the motor home and once into his house, in each case knowing that he is inside. This is reminiscent of poor Jack who, having climbed the beanstalk, finds himself in the house of the Giant. The fact that Chyna faces three challenges is significant in the world of the fairy tale, where three is always a magical number. The repetition of such elements as three wishes, three chances, three guesses, and the like is characteristic, as is the fact that there are often three sons, daughters, or trolls. For example, *Cinderella* has three young girls, the heroine and her two stepsisters.

On her way to confront the ogre, the heroine must pass through an enchanted wood, again a staple of the fairy tale, a form in which forests, woods, and woodsmen abound. In the wood the heroine receives the blessing of magical animals, sometimes in the form of a talking bird or animal, and in this case in the form of the coastal elk, whose mysterious appearance is specifically related to the supernatural when Chyna sees them as angels and Vess as apparitions. The elk appear a total of three times, once in the wood, once at the window of Vess's home, and again as a footprint left in Vess's yard. That they are most surely not creatures familiar to the area is emphasized when Vess's pack of trained killer dobermans does not react to them, suggesting that they carry no scent. Only a magical animal has no scent. The power of the enchanted wood is also invoked three times: once when Chyna first sees the elk, again when the wood is the scene of Vess's firey death, and finally at the end of the book, when Chyna is trying to help Ariel return to a normal life and takes her back into the wood so that she can be healed and thus, symbolically reborn. This circular resurrection pattern is another common element of the fairy tale, as are all forms of magical circles, including characters turning in circles while making three wishes.

Other echoes of fairy tales abound in the novel. When Ariel goes into her catatonic state, she is like Sleeping Beauty, a maiden who is alive but totally unresponsive, just as Ariel is. Vess characterizes Ariel's condition as "magically evasive" (171). Another pervasive element of the fairy tale is the chant said as a charm to ward off evil, and this too appears in *Intensity* in the form of the childhood prayer that Chyna says over and over again to protect herself from the ogre: "Chyna Shepherd, untouched and alive." When Vess hears the chant, it makes him uneasy, as though unconsciously he recognizes its magical power, one that will bring about his destruction. Finally, Vess's horrible death has the graphic detail of the deaths of the orgres in traditional fairy tales, where evil characters come to such horrible endings as being forced to dance in red hot slippers until they die, a fate reserved for Cinderella's step-mother, or being hacked to pieces with an axe, the lot of the wolf in Little Red Riding Hood. True to this tradition, Vess is consumed in a pillar of fire when he steps onto a gasoline flooded roadway and Chyna ignites the fuel. It is indeed an ending suitable for a fairy tale monster.

What makes this fairy tale unusual, and what puts it into the category of a feminist fairy tale, is the casting of a young woman in a role usually reserved for a young man. Usually it is a charming young prince who rescues the fair young maiden, and they marry and live happily ever after. In *Intensity*, there is no charming young prince and no marriage, but there is every indication that there will be a happily ever after ending, with Ariel returning to normalcy and Chyna discovering the meaning of life, all as a result of her adventures in the magic wood and the lair of the ogre. In *Intensity*, young women now have the magical power once reserved for young men, the power of protecting the innocent and of defeating evil.

The dedication to *Intensity* is, like the novel itself, simple and compelling. Koontz writes, "This book is for Florence Koontz. My mother. Long lost. My Guardian." It is most fitting that Koontz should chose the fairy tale as his tribute to his mother, and that he should make the hero of this tale a young woman, who perhaps represents his mother, the person who, he has said, protected him throughout his childhood from the ogre who was his father. Surely any mother would be moved and humbled to be remembered as a guardian and a watcher, a protector of the mythic proportions first described in the simplest, oldest tales we have.

Bibliography

Note: Page numbers referred to in the text are to the paperback editions of Dean Koontz's novels.

WORKS BY DEAN KOONTZ

After the Last Race. New York: Atheneum, 1974.
Anti-Man. New York: Paperback Library, 1970.
The Bad Place. New York: Putnam, 1990.
Beastchild. New York: Lancer, 1970.
Cold Fire. New York: Putnam, 1991.
The Crimson Witch. New York: Curtis, 1971.
Dark of the Woods. New York: Ace, 1970.
The Dark Symphony. New York: Lancer, 1970.
Dark Rivers of the Heart. New York: Knopf, 1994.
Darkfall. New York: Berkeley, 1984.
A Darkness in My Soul. New York: DAW, 1972.
Demon Seed. New York: Bantam, 1973.
Dragon Tears. New York: Putnam, 1993.
The Fall of the Dream Machine. New York: Ace, 1969.
Fear That Man. New York: Ace, 1969.
The Flesh in the Furnace. New York: Bantam, 1972.
Hanging On. New York: M. Evans, 1973.

The Haunted Earth. New York: Lancer, 1973.
Hell's Gate. New York: Lancer, 1970.
Hideaway. New York: Putnam, 1992.
Intensity. New York: Knopf, 1995.
Lightning. New York: Putnam, 1988.
Midnight. New York: Putnam, 1989.
Mr. Murder. New York: Putnam, 1993.
Night Chills. New York: Atheneum, 1976.
Nightmare Journey. New York: Putnam, 1975.
Oddkins. New York: Warner Books, 1988.
Phantoms. New York: Putnam, 1983.
Soft Come the Dragons. New York: Ace, 1970.
Star Quest. New York: Ace, 1968.
Starblood. New York: Lancer, 1972.
Strangers. New York: Putnam, 1986.
Time Thieves. New York: Ace Books, 1972.
Twilight Eyes. Plymouth, Michigan: Land of Enchantment, 1985.
The Vision. New York: Putnam, 1977.
Warlock. New York: Lancer, 1972.
Watchers. New York: Putnam, 1987.
A Werewolf Among Us. New York: Ballantine, 1973.
Whispers. New York: Putnam, 1980.
Winter Moon. New York: Ballantine, 1994.

Writing as David Axton

Prison of Ice. New York: Lippincott, 1976.

Writing as Brian Coffey

Blood Risk. New York: Bobbs-Merrill, 1973.
The Face of Fear. New York: Bobbs-Merrill, 1977.
Surrounded. New York: Bobbs-Merrill, 1974.
The Voice of the Night. New York: Doubleday, 1981.
The Wall of Masks. New York: Bobbs-Merrill, 1975.

Writing as Deanna Dwyer

Children of the Storm. New York: Lancer, 1972.
Dance with the Devil. New York: Lancer, 1973.

The Dark of Summer. New York: Lancer, 1972.
The Demon Child. New York: Lancer, 1971.
Legacy of Terror. New York: Lancer, 1971.

Writing as K. R. Dwyer

Chase. New York: Random House, 1972.
Dragonfly. New York: Random House, 1975.
Shattered. New York: Random House, 1973.

Writing as John Hill

The Long Sleep. New York: Popular Library, 1975.

Writing as Leigh Nichols

The Eyes of Darkness. New York: Pocket Books, 1981.
The House of Thunder. New York: Pocket Books, 1982.
The Key to Midnight. New York: Pocket Books, 1979.
Shadowfires. New York: Avon, 1987.
Twilight. New York: Pocket Books, 1984.

Writing as Anthony North

Strike Deep. New York: Dial, 1974.

Writing as Richard Paige

The Door to December. New York: New American Library, 1985.

Writing as Owen West

The Funhouse. New York: Jove, 1980.
The Mask. New York: Jove, 1981.

Writing as Aaron Wolfe

Invasion. Ontario: Laser Books, 1975.

NONFICTION WRITING AS DEAN KOONTZ

How to Write Best Selling Fiction. Cincinnati: Writer's Digest, 1981.
Writing Popular Fiction. Cincinnati: Writer's Digest, 1972.
———— and Gerda Koontz. *The Pig Society*. Los Angeles: Aware Press, 1970.
———— and Gerda Koontz. *The Underground Lifestyles Handbook*. Los Angeles: Aware Press, 1970.

WORKS ABOUT DEAN KOONTZ

"Dean Ray Koontz." *Contemporary Authors on CD*. Gale Research, 1995.
Feeney, F. X., and Gleick, Elizabeth. "Family Secrets." *People* 28 (Nov. 1994): 141–42.
Greenberg, Martin H., Ed Gorman, and Bill Munster. *The Dean Koontz Companion*. New York: Berkeley, 1994.
Nathan, Paul. "Rights." *Publishers Weekly*, 13 March 1995: 18.
Springen, Karen. "The Cheery Titan of Terror." *Newsweek*, 11 Feb. 1991: 62.
Wiater, Stanley. "Dean R. Koontz in the Fictional Melting Pot." *Writer's Digest*, November 1989: 34–38.

INTERVIEW WITH DEAN KOONTZ

Dean Koontz. "Interview with Dean Koontz," interview by Ed Gorman. In *The Dean Koontz Companion*, edited by Martin H. Greenberg, Ed Gorman, and Bill Munster. New York: Berkeley, 1994: 1–56.

REVIEWS AND CRITICISM

Dark Rivers of the Heart

Rosen, Jay E. Review of *Dark Rivers of the Heart*. *New York Times Book Review*, 13 November 1994: 58.

Mr. Murder

Stade, George. "Monsters Have Needs, Too." Review of *Mr. Murder*. *New York Times Book Review*, 31 October 1993: 18.

Intensity

Blauner, Peter. "Chaining Chyna to a Chair." Review of *Intensity*. *Newsday*, 1 January 1996: 38.

Harrison, Colin. "Murderer's Row." Review of *Intensity*. *New York Times Book Review*, 25 February 1996: 9.

OTHER SECONDARY SOURCES

Abrams, M. H. *A Glossary of Literary Terms*, 3rd ed. New York: Holt, Rinehart, Winston, 1971.

Aldiss, Brian W., with David Wingrove. *Trillion Year Spree: The History of Science Fiction*. New York: Atheneum, 1986.

Cawelti, John G. *Adventure, Mystery and Romance*. Chicago: University of Chicago Press, 1976.

Cuddon, J. A. *The Penguin Dictionary of Literary Terms and Literary Theory*, 3rd ed. London: Penguin Books, 1991.

Dipple, Elizabeth. *Plot*. London: Methuen, 1979.

Holman, C. Hugh, and William Harmon. *A Handbook to Literature*, 6th ed. New York: Macmillan, 1992.

Lynn, Steven. *Texts and Contexts*. New York: HarperCollins, 1994.

Ostrom, Hans. *Lives and Moments: An Introduction to Short Fiction*. Fort Worth: Holt, Rinehart, Winston, 1991.

Rosenberg, Betty, and Diana Tixier Herald. *Genreflecting*. Englewood, Colo.: Libraries Unlimited, 1991.

Ryan, William. "The Genesis of the Techno-Thriller." *Virginia Quarterly Review* 69, no. 1 (1993): 24–40.

Seidman, Michael. "The Suspense/Thriller." *Writer's Digest*, April 1992: 34–35.

Index

About the Author

JOAN G. KOTKER teaches English at Bellevue Community College in Bellevue, Washington. She created and teaches a course on popular literature. Her essays on popular fiction have been published in *It's a Print*; *In the Beginning*; *Women Times Three*; *Encyclopedia of Popular Culture*; *The Oxford Companion to Crime and Mystery Writing*; and *Great Women Mystery Writers* (Greenwood Press, 1994).